Our "Compacted" Compact Clinicals Team

Dear Valued Customer,

Welcome to Compact Clinicals. We are committed to bringing mental health professionals up-to-date, diagnostic and treatment information in a compact, timesaving, easy-to-read format. Our line of books provides current, thorough reviews of assessment and treatment strategies for mental disorders.

We've "compacted" complete information for diagnosing each disorder and comparing how different theoretical orientations approach treatment. Our books use nonacademic language, real-world examples, and well-defined terminology.

Enjoy this and other timesaving books from Compact Clinicals.

Sincerely,

Melanie A. Dean

Melanie Dean, Ph.D.
President

Compact Clinicals Line of Books

Compact Clinicals currently offers these condensed reviews for professionals (order form in back of book):

- **Aggressive and Defiant Behavior:** The Latest Assessment and Treatment Strategies for the Conduct Disorders

- **Attention Deficit Hyperactivity Disorder (in Adults and Children)**: The Latest Assessment and Treatment Strategies

- **Borderline Personality Disorder:** The Latest Assessment and Treatment Strategies

- **Depression in Adults:** The Latest Assessment and Treatment Strategies

- **Obsessive-Compulsive Disorder:** The Latest Assessment and Treatment Strategies

- **Post Traumatic Stress Disorder:** The Latest Assessment and Treatment Strategies

---

Call for Writers

Compact Clinicals is always interested in publishing new titles in order to keep our selection of books current and comprehensive. If you have a book proposal or an idea you would like to discuss, please call or write to:

Melanie Dean, Ph.D., President
Compact Clinicals
7205 NW Waukomis Suite A
Kansas City, MO 64151
(816) 587-0044

Borderline Personality Disorder

The Latest Assessment and Treatment Strategies

second edition

by
Melanie A. Dean, Ph.D.

Compact Clinicals...*condensed reviews for professionals*

Borderline Personality Disorder
The Latest Assessment and Treatment Strategies
second edition
by
Melanie A. Dean, Ph.D.

Published by: Compact Clinicals
                 7205 NW Waukomis Dr.
                 Kansas City, MO 64151
                 816-587-0044

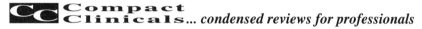

Copyright © 2001 by Dean Psych Press Corp. d/b/a/ Compact Clinicals.
First edition © 1995 by Melanie A. Dean, Ph.D., d/b/a/ Compact Clinicals

Copy Editing by:
       In Credible English
       1800 South West Temple, Suite 501-72
       Salt Lake City, UT 84115
Cover Design by:
       Patrick G. Handley

Library of Congress Cataloging in Publication Data
Dean, Melanie A.
    Borderline personality disorder : the latest assessment and treatment strategies / by Melanie A. Dean.--2nd ed.
    p. ; cm.
    includes bibliographical references and index.
    ISBN 1-887537-17-1 (pbk.)
    1. Borderline personaltiy disorder--Handbooks, manuals, etc.
    {DNLM: 1. Borderline Personaltiy Disorder--diagnosis--Handbooks.
    2. Borderline Personality Disorder--diagnosis--Outlines. 3. Borderline
    Personality Disorder--therapy--Handbooks. 4. Borderline Personality
    Disorder--therapy--Outlines. WM 34 D282b 2001]   1. Title.
    RC569.5 B67 D43 2001
      616.85'852--dc21

                                        00-065754

ISBN 1-887537-17-1

10 9 8 7 6 5 4 3 2 1

Read Me First

As a mental health professional, often the information you need can only be obtained after countless hours of reading or library research. If your schedule precludes this time commitment, Compact Clinicals is the answer.

Our books are practitioner oriented with easy-to-read treatment descriptions and examples. Compact Clinicals books are written in a nonacademic style. Our books are formatted to make the first reading as well as ongoing reference quick and easy. You will find:

- *Anecdotes*—Each chapter begins and ends with a fictionalized account that personalizes the disorder. These accounts include a **"Dear Diary"** entry at the beginning of each chapter that illustrates a typical client's viewpoint about their disorder. Each chapter ends with **"File Notes"** of a fictional therapist, Pat Owen. These **"File Notes"** address assessment, diagnosis, and treatment considerations for the "client writing" the **"Dear Diary"** entries.

- *Sidebars*—Narrow columns on the outside of each page highlight important information, preview upcoming sections or concepts, and define terms used in the text.

- *Definitions*—Terms are defined in the sidebars where they originally appear in the text and in an alphabetical glossary on pages 69 through 72.

- *References*—Numbered references appear in the text following information from that source. Full references appear in a bibliography on pages 73 through 79.

- *Case Examples*—Our examples illustrate typical client comments or conversational exchanges that help clarify different treatment approaches. Identifying information in the examples (e.g., the individual's real name, profession, age, and/or location) has been changed to protect the confidentiality of those clients discussed in case examples.

Contents

Diary of Amy P.

May 4

I went to a therapist today. I can't stop thinking about awful things that could happen to my husband and my kids. I'm spending more and more time undoing and redoing almost everything I do. I'm starting to avoid the next task for fear of getting stuck in this pattern all over again. It's starting to affect my relationships and the amount of work I can handle.

Somebody please help me!

You will be following a typical client's thoughts about their disorder through the "Dear Diary" notes at the beginning of each chapter. At the end of each chapter, a fictional therapist's "File Notes" will reflect the assessment and treatment of the client writing the "Dear Diary" notes.

Chapter One: General Information About Borderline Personality Disorder (BPD)

Millions of Americans suffer from Borderline Personality Disorder (referred to throughout this book as "BPD"), a pervasive pattern of instability that begins early in life and affects most of a person's daily functioning. Written for the professional, this book presents general information about BPD in Chapter One, diagnostic information in Chapter Two, and various theoretical etiologies and treatments including medications, in Chapter Three.

People with BPD suffer from emotional and behavioral instability that begins at an early age and remains persistent throughout their lives. Those with BPD primarily suffer from intense fears that significant others will leave them. Their reactions to these intense fears often include using manipulation, intense anger, and other volatile behaviors to preserve important relationships. In addition, people with BPD fear their need for others. This results in emotional extremes from anger to sadness to euphoria coupled with erratic and often dangerous behavior. Those with BPD typically have one or more addictions (e.g., alcohol, spending money, gambling, drugs, or sex) and frequently respond to their unstable emotions through self mutilation (e.g., cutting on one's self), suicidal thoughts, or suicidal behavior.

BPD symptoms range from mild to very severe. Inpatient psychiatric hospitals often admit people diagnosed with BPD who have extreme symptoms, including suicidal and/or homicidal thoughts or attempts. In an outpatient setting, those with this disorder are likely to have:

- Symptoms of depression
- Suicidal ideation
- Decreased functioning in one or more areas of their lives (e.g., unable to hold a job, marital strife)

The characterization of those with BPD has evolved over several decades with the first written work published in the 1930s. The original document described BPD clients as occupying a continuum between *neurosis* and *psychosis*. The disorder remained vague through the 1940s, and those with BPD were tagged as "pseudoneurotic schizophrenic

---

This chapter will answer the following:

- **How Common is BPD?**—This section discusses prevalence rates in terms of gender, age, and race.

- **What is the Likelihood of Recovery for those with BPD?**—This section discusses prognosis and includes both positive and negative predictors of recovery.

---

neurosis—non-physiological disorder characterized by high levels of anxiety but no impairment in reality testing

psychosis—grossly impaired reality testing

maladaptive behavior
patterns—patterns of
behavior likely to produce so
much psychic distress that
therapy is necessary

(schizotypal personality disorder)." The current definition has changed little and illustrates both the *maladaptive behavior patterns* and the mild psychotic symptoms often displayed by people with BPD.

How Common is BPD?

Calculations of community prevalence rates for BPD range from 2 to 4 percent,[1,2] Based on a U.S. population of approximately 250 million, these statistics indicate that 5 to 10 million people suffer from this disorder. A 1982 cross-cultural study indicated a 15 to 20 percent prevalence rate among psychiatric inpatients.[1] Prevalence rates for outpatient mental health clinics are about 10 percent.[3]

Gender—Women are diagnosed with BPD two to four times more often than men.[4,5] These results may highlight real differences between men and women or result from a labeling difference. Men with similar symptoms are more often diagnosed as having either Antisocial Personality Disorder (APD) or Narcissistic Personality Disorder (NPD).

Age—The highest rates of diagnosed BPD are found between the ages of 19 and 34.[5]

Race—Differences between races in terms of diagnoses suggest that nonwhites are diagnosed as BPD at a significantly higher rate than whites.[5]

What is the Likelihood of Recovery for those with BPD?

The few studies conducted assessing treatment effectiveness indicate a poor, short-term prognosis for those diagnosed with BPD. These studies found chronic symptoms, high relapse rates, poor employment, and poor psychosocial functioning.[6-8] However, research indicates that those with BPD tend to stabilize, contending with fewer BPD symptoms over time. Specifically; dysphoria, impulsiveness, disturbed relationships, and *micropsychotic symptoms* decrease over time, with 75% of cases no longer meeting the criteria for BPD 15 years after initial diagnosis.[9]

micropsychotic symptoms—
minor psychotic symptoms
such as those described on
pages 8 and 9

Completed suicides during the most dysfunctional periods of the disorder range from 3 to 9 percent. Most studies indicate that 9 percent is the more accurate figure.[9,10] This is quite high when compared to the .00011 percent suicide rate among the general U.S. population.[11]

Factors Associated with Completed Suicides in People with BPD[9]

✓ Presence of depression[12]

✓ Mean age of those completing suicide is 32.[9]

✓ Mean time of suicide is four years after inpatient hospitalization.

✓ Those who successfully complete suicide generally:

- Attempted suicide in the past
- Were more highly educated than survivors
- Had fewer psychotic symptoms than survivors
- Reported fewer problems with their mothers than survivors
- Suffered fewer separations and losses before the age of five

✓ No difference exists between people who complete suicide and survivors in terms of age, sex, marital status, conflict with fathers, and substance abuse.

For a discussion on dealing with suicide risks, see pages 16 and 20 through 22.

Factors associated with completed suicides indicate that those with less severe BPD symptomatology and traumatic history have higher suicide rates. Those who completed suicide were more functional in reality testing, more able to form relationships, and more hopeful about the future (as a result of more education). This higher level of functioning may make the emotional struggles related to BPD seem intolerable. Lower functioning people with BPD, that experienced more trauma and difficulty early in life, may have adapted and thus have a higher level of tolerance.

Prognosis Predictors Checklist

Predictors of **positive** prognosis include:[13,14]

- Shorter hospitalizations
- Presence of distract-ibility
- Presence of self-destructive acts during hospitalizations (not self-destructive acts prior to hospitalization)
- Absence of:
    Affective instability
    Parental divorce
    Feelings of entitlement
    Feelings of boredom

Predictors of **negativ e** prognosis include:[13,14]

- Substance abuse
- Prominent antisocial traits
- Dysphoria (mild chronic depression)

Use the Prognostic Predictors Checklist in the side-bar to review indicators of positive and negative outcome. The presence of self-destructive acts during hospitalization is a positive (even if surprising) predictor. This behavior may reflect a readiness to receive help and destructive acting out in such a setting allows clients to learn alternate coping skills.

Therapy Notes
From the Desk of Pat Owen

J.W. (age 22) talked about being diagnosed Antisocial Personality Disorder previously, but seems to me to fit more the pattern of BPD. Complains of poor sleeping, increased alcohol consumption, sexual promiscuity, difficulty concentrating, suicidal ideation, and difficulty in the primary relationship (Alex). Positive note is that previous hospitalization (at age 16) was brief (1 week) and initiated by parents (still mar-ried) due to suicidal ideation. First cutting on self (with a thumbtack, superficial) while in hospital.

Chapter Two: Diagnosing Borderline Personality Disorder

Diary of Jess W.

December 2

Saw my therapist, Pat Owen, today. She's perfect. This time I'm going to get fixed. She wants me to take some tests. Already I feel better. I haven't thought about suicide in days or cutting on myself. Work is bad, though; everybody is out to get me fired. Got back together with Alex; I just know this will last forever.

This chapter will answer the following:

- **What Criteria Are Used for Diagnosing BPD?**—This section reviews DSM-IV diagnostic criteria for BPD.

- **What are Typical Characteristics of Those with BPD?**—This section covers clinical presentation as well as subgroups of BPD.

- **What Tools Are Used for Clinical Assessment?**—This section covers clinical assessment methods including interview questions, self-report measures, and psychometric assessment tools.

- **How is BPD Differentiated from Other Disorders?**—This section helps differentiate BPD from other personality and affective disorders.

What Criteria are Used to Diagnose BPD?

The Diagnostic and Statistical Manual of Mental Disorders-IV (DSM-IV)[3] provides the most current criteria for diagnosing BPD. Much debate exists over the subjectiveness of each criterion. Clinicians should be aware that these criteria define a nonspecific type of serious character pathology rather than a specific, well-defined disorder.[15]

Diagnosis of BPD must reflect observation of ongoing patterns of behavior rather than one time reactions to specific events. Behaviors must lead to functional impairment in the vocational and/or social areas of the person's life.

DSM-IV Criteria for BPD

"A pervasive pattern of instability of mood, interpersonal relationships, self-image and affects, and marked impulsiveness beginning by early adulthood and present in a variety of contexts, as indicated by at least five of the following:

(Continued on Page 6)

idealization—the process whereby the client sees another person as only "good" or "perfect"

devaluation—the process whereby the client undervalues the abilities and/or intentions of others

Diagnostic Note:

Many terms or phrases used in DSM-IV criteria highlight the importance of historical information in diagnosing BPD (e.g., "pervasive," "chronic," "persistent," "frequent," and "pattern of"). Not only must current behavior fit the criteria, historical information must support a long-term pattern of such behavior. If current behavior fits the diagnosis while past behavior does not, then alternate diagnoses need to be considered (e.g., Adjustment Disorder, Affective Disorder, or Psychotic Disorder).

(DSM-IV Criteria, Continued)

1. Frantic efforts to avoid real or imagined abandonment, Note: Do not include suicide or self-mutilating behavior covered in Criterion 5.

2. A pattern of unstable and intense interpersonal relationships characterized by alternating between extremes of *idealization* and *devaluation*.

3. Identity disturbance: markedly and persistently unstable self-image or sense of self.

4. Impulsivity in at least two areas that are potentially self-damaging (e.g., spending, sex, substance abuse, reckless driving, binge eating). Note: Do not include suicide or self-mutilating behavior covered in Criterion 5.

5. Recurrent suicidal behavior, gestures, or threats, or self-mutilation behavior.

6. Affective instability due to a marked reactivity of mood (e.g., intense episodic dysphoria, irritability, or anxiety usually lasting a few hours and only rarely more than a few days).

7. Chronic feelings of emptiness.

8. Inappropriate, intense anger or difficulty controlling anger (e.g., frequent displays of temper, constant anger, recurrent physical fights).

9. Transient, stress-related paranoid ideation or severe dissociative symptoms."

(Reprinted with permission of American Psychiatric Association, Diagnostic and Statistical Manual of Mental Disorders, Fourth Edition, Washington D.C., American Psychiatric Association, 1994.)[3]

Diagnostic Research

Unstable/intense relationships, along with chronic feelings of boredom and emptiness, seem to be the best diagnostic indicators of BPD in an outpatient population.[16] In an inpatient setting, abandonment, unstable relationships, impulsivity and physically self-damaging acts are the best indicators of BPD.[17,18] Of all the diagnostic criteria. stress related paranoia is the least predictive BPD.[18]

When researching clients' past behavioral history, researchers discovered the following commonalities among those with moderate-to-severe BPD:[19]

- Frequent suicide attempts
- Inpatient discharges against medical advice
- First suicide attempt before age 40
- Violence within and outside the hospital
- Gradual deterioration in social and occupational functioning

What are Typical Characteristics of Those with BPD?

During the initial assessment interview and in subsequent treatment sessions, the clinician can recognize BPD clients through several common features:[20,21]

1. ***Disturbance In Self Concept***—People with BPD typically have a highly variable self-image. They generally base their self-image on what others say about them or reactions they receive from others. For example, someone with BPD who receives a critical comment from a coworker may decide, "I am a terrible person." After a compliment, the same person will think, "I am wonderful and perfect." This variability in self-image leads to wide mood swings and contradictory thoughts about one's self.

   The variability in self image is often emotionally painful due to the distress of interpreting experiences negatively and personally. In addition, the

---

Common Features of People with BPD

1. Disturbance in Self Concept
2. Unstable Interpersonal Relationships
3. Cognitive Disturbances
4. Impulsive Behaviors
5. Labile Affect
6. Functional Failures
7. Self-Destructive Acts

---

identity disturbance is associated with a lack of commitment due to values, occupations and relationships fluctuating rapidly along with changes in the person's self-view.[23]

Those with BPD fear separation from others and cannot tolerate feelings of being alone.[20] Sometimes this condition is described as "abandonment depression" leading those with BPD to be socially overactive and compulsive to avoid being alone.[22]

2. ***Unstable Interpersonal Relationships***—People with BPD have a strong need for dependable relationships and are also overly sensitive to others emotions.[24] This sensitivity and dependence on others often results in using indirect and subtle methods for gaining support, such as overidealizing or devaluing the perceived supporter. Those closest to someone with BPD often perceive this behavior as "manipulative" and fail to see the person's underlying needs. Typically, the person with BPD does not consciously admit a need for others and pushes them away during times of stress. This push-and-pull behavior often leads to short-lived relationships, with intense beginnings and endings.

3. ***Cognitive Disturbances***—When dealing with severe stress, people with BPD may suffer from transient psychotic symptoms including *dissociation, derealization, depersonalization,* and *paranoia*.

dissociation—an abnormal psychological state in which one's perception of oneself and/or one's environment is altered significantly

derealization—a sense that one has lost contact with external reality

depersonalization—a sense that one has lost contact with one's own personal reality. For example, a client might relate that, "My body feels strange, like it's not my own."

paranoia—having suspicions and beliefs that one is being followed, plotted against, persecuted, etc.

4. ***Impulsive Behaviors***—*Impulsive* behavior about eating, shopping, and gambling often occur with BPD. The most prevalent impulsive (and *compulsive*) behavior involves alcohol and other drug abuse, especially among young adults.[20,25] Another common impulsive and often addictive behavior is sexual promiscuity or deviance.

5. ***Labile Affect***—People with BPD have sudden, frequent, and intense changes in *affect*.[20,25] Anger, emptiness, loneliness, or abandonment may be expressed as rage or as bitterness and despondency. During times of intense affect, the demands on others for attention and support will likely increase.

Research indicates that those with BPD experience both higher levels of unpleasant emotions and greater fluctuations in pleasant emotions.[26] Specifically, there is often higher rates of anger, hostility and aggressive affects in those with BPD.[27] This labile affect appears to be related to a difficulty in recognizing and regulating emotion. Those with BPD often have lower levels of emotional awareness and less ability to accurately identify emotional facial expressions of others. Additionally, they have less capacity to manage mixed emotions and tend to over respond in intensity to the negative emotions of others.[28] In summary, research indicates that difficulty in regulating emotion is a hallmark dysfunction for those with BPD.

6. *Functional Failures*—Many people with BPD are unable to successfully apply their abilities. They show potential for high achievement; however, their emotional instability and cognitive disturbances prevent them from reaching that potential.

7. *Self-Destructive Activity*—The most extreme self-destructive behavior is suicide (3 to 9 percent of those with BPD complete suicide.)[6] Other self-harm activities include cutting on the body, ingestion of harmful substances, and genital mutilation. Often those with BPD dissociate during self-mutilation and following mutilation feel happier and less dissociative.[29] Additionally, self-destructive behavior overlaps with impulsive behavior on occasion. For example, eating disorders are common among people with BPD.

impulsive—acting without first thinking about the action

compulsive—feeling compelled to act against one's wishes

affect—emotion; feeling; mood

labile affect—marked and rapid mood shifts

hyperphrasia—pathologically excessive talking

delusion—a belief that is maintained despite much evidence or argument to the contrary

referential thinking—believing others' actions or external events are specifically related to you when they are not

hallucinations—hearing or seeing things others do not

mild formal thought disorder—disturbances in speech, communication, and/or thinking

Subgroups of BPD

People diagnosed with BPD may appear very different from each other. These variations reflect three primary subgroups:

• Those who are primarily depressed
• Those who are primarily impulsive
• Those whose symptoms are primarily psychotic

These subgroups are not mutually exclusive; clients can manifest symptoms from one or all of the subgroups. The chart below presents these subgroups in terms of symptoms and related disorders.

Subgroup— BPD with...	Symptoms	Related Disorders*
Primarily: Depressed	Chronic depression A demanding, dramatic interpersonal style Atypical depressive symptoms of reactivity, lability, rejection-sensitivity, **hyperphrasia**# and hypersomnia	Major depression, atypical depression, and dysthymia
Primarily: Impulsive	Overdose Suicide threats Self-mutilation Alcohol or other drug binges Sexual promiscuity Antisocial acts	Bipolar affective disorder, cyclothymia disorder, antisocial personality disorder, organic disorders (including post traumatic disorder, seizure-associated and attention deficit hyperactivity disorder)
Primarily: Psychotic**	**Paranoia**# **Referential thinking**# **Depersonalization**# & **Derealization**# **Delusions**# **Hallucinations**# Odd experiences **Mild Formal Thought Disorder**#	Schizotypal personality disorder, brief reactive psychosis, and atypical psychosis

* These represent disorders with which there is a high dual diagnosis and/or correlation of symptoms with BPD.

** Multiple stress-related, psychotic-like symptoms are usually transient. Psychotic-like symptoms are most often mood congruent (e.g., paranoid ideation or referential thinking clients would have depressive and poor self-image content congruent with their depressive mood.) Brief, supportive hospitalizations are often sufficient to control these symptoms.

\# In this table, the words that are **followed by a "#" sign** were defined on the previous pages.

What Tools are Used for Clinical Assessment?

Several tools can help the clinician diagnose BPD including the Clinical Interview, Self-Report (Interview) Instruments, and Psychometric Assessment Tools.

Clinical Interview

During the initial interview, the clinician needs to specifically ask about certain factors that can help diagnose BPD, such as:

- Historical patterns of substance abuse, gambling, money-spending binges, or promiscuity (indications of impulsive symptoms).

- Intense beginnings and endings of relationships and cutoff relationships with family members (indicators of unstable relationships).

- Suicide attempts, self-mutilation, binging and purging, or not eating (indicators of self-destructive behavior).

- Psychotic-like symptoms such as depersonalization, derealization, delusions, hallucinations, paranoia, and referential thinking. Check for the duration and frequency of these experiences as they are usually transient during times of stress.

- History of sexual, physical, or emotional abuse. Many people with BPD have experienced significant trauma.

Self-Report (Interview) Instruments

Interview instruments available to assess and diagnose BPD include:

1. *Diagnostic Interview for Borderline Personality Disorders-Revised (DIB-R)*[30]— Based on DSM-III-R criteria, this instrument has strong *sensitivity* and *specificity* for diagnosis. The DIB-R reliably distinguishes BPD from other Axis II personality

sensitivity ratio—cases correctly diagnosed

specificity ratio—non-cases correctly identified

disorders. It consists of a one-hour, semi-structured interview focusing on social adaptation, self-destructive impulsiveness, depressive and angry affect, *dissociative ego states,* and interpersonal relations.

dissociative ego states—attitudes and emotions that produce anxiety become separated from the rest of the person's personality and function independently.

2. ***Structured Clinical Interview for DSM-III-R Personality Disorders (SCID-II)***[31]—Designed as a guide for diagnostic interviewing using DSM-III-R criteria, the SCID-II contains sections for both Axis I and II disorders. The Axis II portion of the interview includes diagnostic questions for 11 different DSM-III-R personality disorders. This instrument demonstrates strong *validity* and *interrater reliability.*[32]

validity—degree that the instrument measures what it reports to measure

interrater reliability—degree that different raters agree on a diagnosis based on the use of the instrument

3. ***Personality Assessment Inventory (PAI)***—This 344 item inventory has 22 scales including validity, clinical, treatment and interpersonal scales including four borderline feature subscales; Affective Instability, Identity Problems, Negative Relationships, and Self-Harm. This instrument has good reliability and validity data and can also be used for diagnosing BPD.[33,34]

4. ***Borderline Personality Inventory*** — This instrument is based on a psychodynamic formulation of BPD, while also compatible with DSM-IV diagnostic criteria. It assesses Identity Diffusion, Primitive Defense Mechanisms, Reality Testing, and Fear of Closeness. In addition to the descriptive validity scales, a cutoff score can be used to diagnose BPD. The instrument shows good reliability, sensitivity, and specificity data for diagnosis.[35]

5. ***Objective Behavioral Index*** —assesses treatment response in clients with sever personality disorders. It measures dysfunctional behaviors as well as use of mental health services.[36]

Instruments for assessing suicide and self-harm

Self Harm Inventory (SHI)—This instrument identifies self destructive behaviors and is useful as a screening tool for BPD. It is a 22 item semi-structured inventory showing preliminary validity for diagnosis.[37]

Beck Scale for Suicide Ideation — This scale is a self administered 21 item scale assessing frequency and content of suicidal ideation for therapist follow-up.[38]

Suicide Probability Scale (SPS) — This is a 36 item self administered scale offering a suicide probability score. It also provides more detailed information on four subscales of Hopelessness, Suicide Ideation, Negative Self Evaluation, and Hostility.[39]

See page 16 for a discussion on assessing suicide risk.

Psychometric Assessment Tools

Psychometric instruments commonly used to aid in diagnosis include:

* Minnesota Multiphasic Personality Inventory (MMPI)
* Wechsler Adult Intelligence Scale-Revised (WAIS-R)
* Rorschach
* Millon Clinical Multi-Axial Inventory-II (MCMI)

Minnesota Multiphasic Personality Inventory-Second Edition (MMPI-2)—The MMPI-2[40] is a widely used instrument assessing personality and symptoms of distress. This test consists of 567 statements that the client rates as either true or false. Clinicians score the test, often electronically, and construct a profile based on several specific scales.

Research findings suggest that those with BPD score high on both the "neurotic" (scales 1-4) and the "psychotic" (scales 6-8) MMPI scales. There is no clear pattern of MMPI-2 results that distinguishes BPD from other disorders. Commonalities among BPD profiles include an elevated F scale

MMPI Scales
L: Lie Scale
F: Fake Bad
K: Clinical Defensiveness
1: Hypochondriasis
2: Depression
3: Hysteria
4: Psychopathic Deviate
5: Masculinity/Femininity
6: Paranoia
7: Psychasthenia
8: Schizophrenia
9: Hypomania
0: Social Introversion

There are numerous books available to help interpret MMPI test results; the most frequently used are Graham[41] and Greene.[42]

and an overall elevated profile (or "floating profile").[43] Typically, high scales are 2, 4, and 6 through 8.[17,33,43] Some research indicates that scales F and 8 are almost always elevated and that scales L and K are typically less than 50.[44]

Wechsler Adult Intelligence Scale (WAIS-R)—The WAIS-R, like many other intelligence tests, was developed to:

- Measure the client's intellectual potential
- Obtain clinically relevant information pertaining to the client's decision-making capacity
- Determine the ability to process language
- Assess the functional integrity of the brain [45]

Rappaport's 1945 study led many to believe that those with BPD perform well on structured tests, such as the WAIS-R. The same study indicated that these people performed poorly, often with signs of thought disorder, on unstructured projective tests.[46] Subsequent studies do not support this research.[44] Typical WAIS-R results for BPD clients show few instances of thought disorder, relatively intact Picture Completion, and easy errors on Comprehension questions. People with BPD show a wide range of WAIS-R profiles.[44]

projective measure of personality (as measured by the Rorschach)—the stimuli or inkblots are assumed to be neutral; they were created randomly and have no specific shape nor function. Shapes, movement, and other elements of the pictures that clients see in the blots are a product of the client's own experiences and perceptual orientation projected on the cards.

Rorschach—This test is a *"projective" measure of personality*. It consists of ten cards with randomly created inkblots, some in monochrome and some in color. The clinician shows the cards to the client one at a time, records the answers, and later scores them.

Although many systems score and interpret responses to the Rorschach test, the most widely used is the Exner Method, a comprehensive system for administering, scoring, and interpreting Rorschach results.[47] This is probably the best system to use for two reasons:

1. The Exner Method's large normative base allows the clinician to determine the irregularity of a particular score.

2. This system has survived extensive research on its validity and utility.

No simple profile has been identified for Rorschach findings when used to diagnose BPD. However, scores for those with BPD seem to show:[44]

- Poorer capacity for behavior control (indicated by lower D scores).[43]

- More involvement with the self at the expense of in-depth involvement with others (indicated by a higher egocentricity index).[43]

- Evidence of minimum to moderate thought disorder with little to no evidence of severe thought disorder [demonstrated by few if any CONTAM (contamination), ALOG (autistic logic) and FABCOM (fabulized combination) scores]. High CONTAM scores successfully distinguish schizophrenics from those with BPD because that score almost exclusively predicts schizophrenia.[43]

- Emotional overload or withdrawal (demonstrated by higher affective ratios).[43]

- Poor perceptual accuracy (indicated by approximately 69% good Form Quality).[43]

- Impaired capacity to regulate emotional arousal (demonstrated by high Sum of Shading and Color responses).[43]

Millon Clinical Multi-Axial Inventory-II (MCMI-II)—This self-report questionnaire assesses personality disorders for inpatients and is based on Millon's *taxonomy* for personality disorders.[48] However, the inventory provides inadequate *convergent* or *discriminate validity* for DSM Axis II personality disorders. MCMI-II fails to effectively diagnose BPD because Millon's theoretical orientation to personality disorders does not parallel DSM criteria.

> The information presented on Rorschach scores is intended for professionals trained in interpreting Rorschach results.

> *taxonomy*—classification system

> *convergent validity*—when test results positively correlate with other instruments measuring BPD

> *discriminate validity*—an instrument's ability to discriminate BPD from other disorders

Refer to pages 20 through 22 for a discussion on how to respond to suicide potential in BPD clients.

Suicide Assessment

During initial and ongoing therapeutic discussions, the clinician must assess the BPD client's suicide potential.

Factors that indicate a greater risk of suicidal behavior include:[49]

- *Previous suicide attempts that have been lethal in nature*—An indication of greater suicidal risk might be a serious overdose attempt (rather than ingestion of a dozen aspirin), or deep cutting on the wrists (versus superficial scratches).

- *The specificity of the suicide plan*—A client that has worked out the time, circumstances, and means of committing suicide is more at risk than the client who has no plan but admits to thinking about suicide.

- *The level of commitment to suicide and the availability of instruments*—A client who reports a "decision" to commit suicide is at greater risk than a client who reports "thinking" about suicide. In addition, someone who wants to overdose and has pills at home is more at risk than someone without their chosen method of suicide readily available.

- *The level of impulsivity*—A client who generally exhibits impulsive behaviors in areas such as gambling, spending money, or beginning and ending relationships, is at greater risk for acting on their suicidal thoughts. The greater the impulsivity, the greater the suicide risk.[51]

- *The level of substance use*—The use of substances, particularly alcohol, leads to disinhibition and therefore greater risk for suicide, particularly with unplanned suicide attempts.[52]

- *The level of social support available*—People who have supportive friends and family to rely upon are less likely to act on suicidal ideation.

Predisposing Factors to Greater Suicide Risks[12,50,51]

- Being depressed
- Living alone
- Being unmarried
- Being unemployed
- Having experienced recent loss
- Presenting a history of early parental loss
- History of childhood abuse
- Having a family history of suicide
- Having been recently discharged from hospitalization
- Having a severe physical illness
- Having a recent social failure

How is BPD Differentiated from Other Disorders?

The BPD diagnostic category overlaps with other personality disorders, especially affective disorders, narcissistic, antisocial, histrionic, schizotypal personality disorders and Post Traumatic Stress Disorder.[4] The table below differentiates each of these disorders from BPD.

Antisocial Personality Disorder (APD)	• Those with BPD may perform antisocial acts, but are more likely to feel personal shame or remorse than those with APD. • People with APD usually regret their actions only because of the consequences to themselves, not others. • Antisocial acts committed by people with BPD are usually viewed as survival issues, and the individual experiences uncomfortable anxiety as a result. Those with APD usually feel no anxiety about their antisocial behavior.
Histrionic Personality Disorder (HPD)	• Those with HPD have a higher overall functional level, display greater employment and relationship stability, and maintain a more stable self-image than those with BPD. • Those with HPD do not commit the repeated self-destructive acts characteristic of those with BPD.[6]
Narcissistic Personality Disorder (NPD)	• Those with BPD openly express their need for support in interpersonal relationships while narcissistics are more subtle. • Those with NPD typically deny their many dependency needs. They are better able to have consistent and sustained relationships. People with BPD have more extreme affective displays and less stable relationships. • NPD clients demonstrate grandiosity in contrast to the devalued sense of self that is evident in people with BPD.[2]
Schizotypal Personality Disorder	• The flat affect that often accompanies BPD with depression is usually temporary or state-like (it lifts as the depression lifts). Flat affect is stable or trait-like for those with SPD. • Clinicians view the psychotic symptoms present in those with SPD to be more trait-like, while those with BPD demonstrate similar symptoms that are more transient, stress-related, or state-like.[53] • Those with BPD have significantly higher rates of depression, as well as drug and alcohol abuse compared to those with SPD.[53]
Affective Disturbance (Depression, Dysthymia, Bipolar Disorder)	• Some researchers argue that BPD is a part of the affective disturbance spectrum. Others highlight the overlap between BPD and affective disturbance.[6] • People who have affective instability, but who function well with minimal support and intervention, likely suffer from an affective disorder and would not meet the BPD criteria.

Researchers have found that even with consensus of multiple raters on the diagnosis of BPD, 60 percent meet the criteria for other disorders as well.[16,54,55] Particularly:

- Anxiety Disorders
- Mood Disorders
- Substance Abuse
- Eating Disorders

Differentiating BPD from Other Disorders, Continued

Post Traumatic Stress Disorder	• Those with BPD have often experienced significant trauma; however, they do not as a matter of course, experience PTSD symptoms such as hypervigilance, exaggerated startle response, flashbacks, intrusive recollections, or efforts to avoid trauma related thoughts and feelings.
	• The dissociative symptoms associated with PTSD are a direct result of trauma related stimuli rather than general stress related dissociative symptoms seen with BPD.
	• Many people with BPD also suffer from PTSD.

Therapy Notes
From the Desk of Pat Owen

Recommended psychological testing of MMPI and Rorschach today. Previous testing shows average intelligence. Gathered more history during interview of suicide gestures (overdosed on aspirin at age 12, superficial cutting of wrists at age 14, and suicide threat at age 18). Passive suicide behaviors of doing drugs (Cannabis, amphetamines) since age 14. Symptoms of referential and paranoid thinking at work (believes being set up to be fired). Complains of depersonalization ("Can't feel my body."). Idealization of me and significant other (Alex) today as well as voicing fears of abandonment (i.e., "I know you and Alex will never leave me.").

Chapter Three: Treating Borderline Personality Disorder

Diary of Jess W.

February 18

Individual therapy has really helped; now, my therapist wants me to do group therapy. I think I will. Alex took our talk well last night. I told her I was angry and we talked about what happened. I can't believe I was able to talk to her so well about my anger rather than go out and pick up someone or cut on myself. I really have made progress. I think group therapy will be helpful too.

What are the Global Treatment Issues Related to BPD?

Perhaps the most crucial issue for therapists treating clients with BPD is the potential for suicide. Therapists have an ethical obligation to intervene to prevent clients from committing suicide. This section discusses how to respond to the suicide potential inherent in treating BPD, as well as considerations and treatment goals for inpatient hospitalization.

What are Possible Responses to the Suicide Potential Inherent in Treating People with BPD?

Therapists must document how they assess the suicide potential of their BPD clients and what intervention strategies they employ.

This chapter will answer the following:

- **What are the Global Treatment Issues Related to BPD?**—This section discusses how to respond to the suicide potential inherent in treating BPD, considerations for inpatient hospitalization, and inpatient treatment goals.

- **What are the Environmental Influences that May Cause BPD?**—This section addresses each theoretical treatment approach in terms of goals, rationale, treatment guidelines, sample dialogs between therapist and client, and a review of efficacy research.

- **What are the Biological Influences that May Cause BPD?**—This section deals with the biological theories for the origin of BPD, the psychopharmacological treatment approaches utilized, and an overview of efficacy research.

Outpatient intervention strategies used to structure and confine the client's suicidal behavior include:

- Exploring the factors leading to the suicide crisis and helping the client decide not to commit suicide.

- Negotiating a "life-preserving" or "no-suicide" contract with the client. This contract may be negotiated for specific periods of time (e.g., 24 hours) or until the next therapy appointment.

- Reaching an agreement with clients for the therapist to contact their family or significant others to obtain support for them. Additionally, the therapist makes a contract with clients that specifies their willingness to utilize their support group during the crisis.

Therapists must use inpatient intervention strategies if the client is at high risk for suicide. When treating people with BPD on an outpatient basis, therapists need to make advance arrangements to admit their clients to a hospital should an immediate need arise. Special considerations for voluntary and involuntary hospitalization include:

- *Voluntary Hospitalization*—The therapist facilitates the client's entry into a hospital or helps the client take the steps necessary to enter a hospital. Many therapists believe the choice of hospital and means of entry need to be discussed with the client at the beginning of the therapeutic relationship so the client knows what to expect in case of hospitalization.

- *Involuntary Hospitalization*—If the client refuses to be hospitalized voluntarily, the therapist must involuntarily hospitalize the client, including making necessary arrangements for transportation.

Consultation with the hospital and with other colleagues can help the therapist decide whether hospitalization will best protect the client. In fact, many clients may benefit from joining these consultations to witness problem-solving strategies and take part in reducing their own anxiety.

Many people with BPD have chronic suicidal thoughts that are part of a consistent mode of relating to themselves and others.[50] They often try to have others assume responsibility for their suicidal behavior, thus consistently avoiding personal responsibility. In such cases, the therapist must evaluate the seriousness of the suicide potential and weigh intervention against assuming too much responsibility for the clients' behavior.

What are the Most Important Considerations for Inpatient Hospitalization?

Therapists must consider several factors when deciding to hospitalize a client. The results of several studies have led many professionals to carefully weigh the negative effects that inpatient hospitalization may have versus the threat of self-harm. Some argue that hospitalization may lead people with BPD to "rapidly develop apparently hospital-induced behaviors more severe than the disturbances that led to their admission in the first place."[56] Some theorists believe that regression (reverting to a more childlike pattern of behavior) results when the inpatient treatment plan includes more structure than is necessary to protect the client and preserve the treatment.[57]

To overcome these potentially negative effects of hospitalization, inpatient hospital staff should focus on:[58]

- Stabilizing the client in regard to self-harm behaviors
- Restoring the client's ability to do reality testing
- Initiating a detailed plan for outpatient treatment
- Resolving treatment impasses

A physician should evaluate the client to determine the need for psychotropic medications.

Stabilization often involves the use of a workable contract between the client, the therapist, and hospital staff. Various theorists agree that inpatient treatment contracts for clients with BPD should:[59]

1. Be agreed upon by all parties and specify focused, achievable goals and the therapeutic strategies to reach the goals.

Characteristics Common Among those Hospitalized with BPD

Research has found that BPD clients hospitalized had certain characteristics different from those treated strictly as outpatients.[59] According to this studies, inpatients with BPD were:

- Mostly female

- Had a higher occupational status

- Experienced frequent unemployment

- Had a lower probability of entering or sustaining a marriage

- Were more likely to be admitted voluntarily

- Had extensive treatment histories that began early in life

- Were frequently self-destructive

- Were more likely to have been treated with anti-anxiety and antidepressant medications

---

Patient characteristics associated with multiple hospitalizations for those with BPD include:
- anorexia
- psychotic symptoms
- suicidality

2. Assign specific responsibilities to all parties, including client and staff, and set limits on certain behaviors, including self-harm behavior.

3. Provide the minimum degree of structure necessary for client and treatment safety.

4. Specify staff availability and other resources for the client as alternate means of managing intolerable feelings.

5. Emphasize positive reinforcement for appropriate behavior (such as earning one-on-one time with staff).

6. Be generated at a constructive time, not when the staff have unresolved punitive feelings toward the client.

7. Be strictly enforced but allow for reasonable, negotiated modifications.

What are the Environmental Influences that May Cause BPD?

Research supports an environmental influence for BPD through a variety of familial markers. Such research finds that the majority (up to 91 percent) of people with BPD have experienced significantly higher rates of childhood trauma than non-BPD clients.[61,64] Other research indicates that people with BPD are more likely than those without BPD to report early separation experiences and neglect primarily in the form of emotional withdrawal from early caregivers.[63,64]

Additionally, adults with BPD versus those without BPD, experience significantly more violence such as physical abuse from a partner or recent physical or sexual assault. Four risk factors have been found to predict those with BPD who are adult victims of violence. These are:[65]
- female gender
- substance abuse disorder
- childhood sexual abuse
- childhood experience of emotional withdrawal by a caretaker

Familial Markers That Indicate an Environmental Influence for BPD.[61,62]

Environmental Influence Factor Reported	% of BPD Clients Reporting Each Factor
Physical Abuse	71
Sexual Abuse	68
Witnessed Serious Domestic Violence	62

Clients who experienced childhood sexual abuse perpetrated by a parent, tend to engage in more self-destructive behaviors such as suicide and self-mutilation.[66]

There are numerous theories (many that overlap) regarding the environmental causes of and individual treatments for BPD. The following briefly describes the various environmental theories presented in greater detail later in this chapter.

Families of those with BPD have a higher incidence of borderline-type behaviors,[67] alcoholism,[68] Antisocial Personality Disorder,[62,69] and other personality disorders.[70,71]

1. ***Psychodynamic Approach***—This approach seeks to produce broad-based character change in which clients gain control of their overwhelming emotions. This control process (also referred to as ego mastery) allows the clients the capacity to form stable relationships and maintain an integrated sense of self.[72]

Environmental Approaches to the Origin of BPD Include:
• Psychodynamic
• Psychoanalytic
• Interpersonal
• Cognitive
• Dialectical Behavior Therapy
• Cognitive Analytic Therapy
• Relapse Prevention Therapy
• Group Therapy

2. ***Psychoanalytic Approach***—Psychoanalytic theorists view BPD as developmental in nature. These theorists believe that people with BPD experienced early trauma that has frustrated or inhibited normal developmental growth. This trauma has kept the person at a "primitive" (or childlike) level of psychic functioning.

3. ***Interpersonal Psychotherapy (IPT)***—This approach is based on the theory of personality developed by H.S. Sullivan.[73] This theory defines personality as a relatively enduring pattern of recurrent interpersonal situations. IPT assumes that interpersonal interactions shape current behavior. Consequently, disordered behavior or communications are a result of disordered interpersonal relations.

IPT's focus on interpersonal interactions presents a marked contrast to the psychoanalytic view that intrapsychic conflicts are expressed on an interpersonal level.

4. ***Cognitive Therapy***—This theory assumes that dysfunction stems from maladaptive *schemas*. These maladaptive schemas result in biased judgements that lead clients to consistently rationalize their own dysfunctional behavior and to be unable to test their interpretations against reality. For example, this approach views people with BPD as holding unrealistic expectations

schemas—organized belief systems that attach meaning to events regarding current interpersonal relationships based on rigid beliefs about relationships with early primary caregivers.

5. *Dialectical Behavior Therapy (DBT)*—These theorists stress the relationship between biological and environmental forces. For example, this theory sees the person with BPD as biologically predisposed to being vulnerable to emotional extremes while being influenced by an emotionally invalidating environment.

6. *Cognitive Analytic Therapy (CAT)* — This section provides a brief overview of a relatively new therapy that helps clients identify and alter recipro-cal relationship roles learned through early child-hood experiences.

7. *Relapse Prevention*—The relapse prevention model is a social learning model that does not specifically address people with BPD. However, it is a theoretical model for treating people who struggle with addictions. Since people with BPD often have one or more addictions or compulsive behaviors based on immediate gratification, the components of relapse prevention represent important considerations for treatment.

8. *Group Psychotherapy*—This section provides the rationale and benefits for using group therapy with BPD clients rather than specific guidelines on interventions and techniques. The information presented is written for those already experienced in conducting group treatment or those who are planning to refer a client to group therapy.

What is the Psychodynamic Approach to Treating BPD?

Psychodynamic approaches seek to help clients gain insight into past unmet emotional needs that influence their currently dysfunctional behavior. These approaches help them identify more direct and appropriate ways to meet their emotional needs. Most psychodynamic approaches focus on the client's past relationships to help modify current relationships. However, Kernberg et. al., who developed the expressive psychotherapy approach, support the primary focus of therapy being on "here and now" relationships as a means of interpreting and changing behavior. More traditional psycho-dynamic approaches focus on the past.[72]

Object Relations theorists maintain that the main problem for people with BPD is that they failed to mature psychologically to a point where they can differentiate between self and other. Because they are stuck at this developmental level, BPD clients shift their identity and feelings based on how others react to them. This lack of differentiation of self from others is also related to an inability to balance positive and negative feelings, such as love and aggression.

Object Relations theories represent one school of thought within psychodynamic theories.

Kernberg et. al. attribute this lack of integration of positive and negative feelings to abundant pathological aggression within the BPD client. This aggression may be biological in nature or it may be a reaction to an early frustrating environment.[22]

What are Commonly Used Defense Mechanisms?

Those with BPD commonly use several defense mechanisms, including *splitting, projective identification*, idealization, and *denial*. These defense mechanisms keep the person with BPD from developing more integrated, useful coping mechanisms. Without these coping mechanisms, the person experiences a general "free floating anxiety," lack of impulse control, and occasional periods of transient psychotic processes.[22]

Splitting happens when people separate themselves and others into "good" and "bad" categories. This view protects BPD sufferers from recognizing their own aggressive impulses. It also allows them to preserve "good" memories of themselves

splitting—the division of self and others into "all good" or "all bad" categories, which results in sudden reversals of feelings and conceptualizations about one's self and others[73]

projective identification— the process whereby the client behaves toward others in such a manner that elicits the very behavior that will confirm their own underlying beliefs

denial—the process whereby the client responds to an event as if it is not or has not happened

and their primary caregiver rather than feel rage toward their early primary caregiver for not meeting their needs.

Those with BPD who use **projective identification,** typically elicit the precise behaviors in others that confirm the clients' underlying beliefs. For example, they may accuse the therapist of not caring and not listening. These accusations, usually voiced quite strongly, will likely produce feelings of anger in the therapist. The therapist's angry feelings will then be interpreted by clients as confirmation that the therapist is uncaring, not listening, and not trustworthy to meet their emotional needs.

Idealization allows clients to disavow the therapist's inability to perfectly meet their needs. Because of splitting, clients are unable to recognize that someone who is unable to meet all of their needs can still meet some of their needs.

The counterpart of idealization is **devaluation,** which is the perception that others are persecutory or dangerous and thus completely unable to meet their needs.

For BPD clients, **denial** can be a very strong defense mechanism, strong enough to let clients deny events that they witness. Denial serves the purpose of defending clients' fragile view of themselves and others.

How do I Treat BPD Using a Psychodynamic Approach?

The goal of psychodynamic therapy is to help clients identify their feelings (e.g., rage) and identify to what those feelings are a reaction. In this process of identifying the feelings and situation, the client and therapist can view current events as reflections of past events in which similar needs have gone unmet.

intrapsychic—psychological processes within a person

Psychodynamic treatment seeks to make characterological changes and assumes that the person's behavior is motivated by *intrapsychic* conflicts that are highly individualized. Psychodynamic methods include traditional exploratory, insight-oriented approaches, as well as supportive and expressive approaches. For each of these approaches, there are several shared views, such as:

- The initial therapy session needs to focus on clarifying the role of the therapist and the client, as well as developing a structure for treatment. When the client deviates from the therapy contract, there is a framework for interpreting the actions. For example, contracts that call for a commitment to attend therapy sessions provide a groundwork for exploring the feelings and thoughts that led to a particular absence.

• To establish vital structure, therapists must define the limits of their intervention for self-destructive behavior. For example, the therapist may set up a contract with clients that they will seek help at hospital emergency rooms for suicidal or other self-destructive behaviors.

Setting up a shared responsibility for therapy sessions and providing a framework for therapy interactions is vital to the success of therapy. To accomplish this shared responsibility, clients must keep track of and relay their own thoughts and feelings related to pertinent impulses and behavior. The therapist then helps them to explore and understand the connection between their thoughts and feelings related to behavior.

Traditional Psychodynamic Treatment—A leading proponent of exploratory, insight-oriented psychodynamic therapy, Pollack has developed a treatment approach that highlights traditional psychodynamic therapy and adds a focus on the developmental process. This integrated developmental-psychodynamic, psychotherapeutic approach includes three phases of treatment: Holding, Understanding, and Moving On.[74]

1. *Holding*—This phase entails helping clients to perceive the therapist as a reliable and consistent person who can be depended upon to accept their overt and underlying feelings, including their sadness and rage. BPD clients have not likely experienced a positive, holding relationship in the past and, while they long for such a relationship, they are suspicious of it at the same time. The therapist's ability to empathetically accept this difficulty in trusting will be the most helpful in changing their suspicions. By modifying these suspicions, clients can begin to accept their own ambivalent feelings for the therapist that range

The treatment examples on page 30 demonstrate the differences between the traditional, supportive, and expressive approaches to psychodynamic treatment methods for people with BPD. These examples respond to the same initial comment by the client.

Building the client/therapist relationship is the most important and therapeutic activity at this early stage of treatment.

Sometimes the therapist will need to allow the client the opportunity to experience and express their rage; other times the therapist may need to react by clarifying the situation and setting limits in order to preserve the relationship and the safety of the client.

from idealization to devastation and rage. The therapist must withstand these extreme emotional expressions and reflect on the loneliness and sense of loss that clients must feel.

2. *Understanding*—This phase requires the therapist to help clients explore their own developmental history and pain. Research indicates that people with BPD often experience very real trauma and abuse as children that affects later adult function- ing.[75] Helping clients connect past feelings to their current suspiciousness and feelings increases understanding and decreases the sense of discon- nectedness that clients feel with themselves. During this phase, the therapist can help clients understand their behaviors (e.g., dissociation, self- destructive behaviors, rageful enactments) as being functional defense maneuvers they once used to protect themselves. Clients can then come to empathize with their own needs and feel more connected with themselves.

3. *Moving On*—In this phase, the therapist helps clients recognize that they can understand, empa- thize, and soothe themselves. Additionally, clients become aware that mature interdependence on significant others is necessary for psychological and emotional balance. The therapist supports and encourages clients in this balance of autonomy and affiliation with others.

Supportive Psychodynamic Therapy—Some clinicians and researchers report that the best treatment approach for people with BPD is supportive psychodynamic therapy. The focus of supportive therapy is to:

1. Help the client establish and maintain a psycho- therapeutic relationship
2. Support and strengthen defenses
3. Avoid *regression* in the treatment process

This approach assumes that, by having a sustained relation- ship, the client is better able to "order their chaotic inner

During therapy, the experi- ences in daily life and in the therapeutic relationship will remind the client of past disappointments, mostly related to separation.

Supportive therapy, which focuses on the healing nature of the client/ therapist relationship, emphasizes problem-solving rather than interpretation.

regression—reverting or retreating into an earlier, more childlike pattern of behavior

28

experiences and consequently gain stability in their daily life functions."[6] Treatment is generally structured with clear goals and much direction from the therapist with the focus on current functional relationship factors including warmth, consistency, and availability of the therapist.

This approach favors education and problem-solving over confrontation and interpretation. This sometimes contrasts with the more traditional psychodynamic approaches which intervene directly to change personality organization.

Expressive Psychodynamic Therapy—Though Kernberg developed a program using supportive therapy, he tends to advocate the use of expressive, insight-oriented therapy that focuses on the here and now instead of the past.[72,76] Kernberg asserts that clients must face and bear those aspects of their inner life against which they focus their strongest defense mechanisms. Expressive therapy stresses that only by facing and understanding one's inner self can true structural change take place.

How Effective is Psychodynamic Therapy for Treating BPD?

A randomized controlled study of psychodynamic group oriented therapy in a partial hospitalization program yielded positive results. A group of clients with a mixture of personality disorders, including many with BPD, met over the course of 18 weeks. Positive treatment gains included improvements in interpersonal functioning, self-esteem, life satisfaction and defensive functioning that were maintained at the eight month follow up assessment.[78]

Naturalistic studies conducted by the Menninger Clinic and others suggest possible advantages to conducting expressive therapy combined with *environmental structuring* over a supportive therapy approach.[79,80] Subsequent research indicates that most therapists eventually shift toward more supportive therapy techniques after initially working with intensive interpretive strategies. These results also indicate that the more supportive strategies are able to bring about basic changes in personality.[81]

Those that consider supportive therapy to be the treatment of choice believe that internal structural changes and behavioral change can be brought about through the healing aspects of the therapeutic relationship itself.[77]

naturalistic studies— observation and documentation of therapy in the natural setting

environmental structuring—setting guidelines, limits, and rules for the process of therapy

Psychodynamic Treatment Examples (Client=C Therapist=T)

C₁: Last time we met I could tell you didn't really care about me, you were just seeing me for the money. I was so mad I went home and cut on my wrists. I couldn't help myself.

Traditional Approach

T₁: In what way did it feel like I didn't really care about you?

C₂: When I was talking about my mom being so angry you started taking notes...you weren't really listening...I'm just another case to you.

T₂: You have a lot of strong feelings about this.

C₃: You bet! I felt so mad. You're supposed to care and listen. I knew all along that you really didn't.

T₃: Is this a familiar feeling?

C₄: Yeah, my mom used to ignore me and wouldn't listen. I'd get so mad; it's like I wasn't even there.

T₄: It sounds like I reminded you of your mom last week?

C₅: Yeah, women really can't be trusted. Men are the only ones that can really be trusted.

T₅: In the past, how did you deal with all that anger about your mom not listening to you?

C₆: I used to just go in my room; I'd be so mad that the only way I could calm myself down was to cut [on wrist and leg].

T₆: You did the same thing last week. Sounds like it is very important for you to be listened to.

C₇: Yeah. I hate someone not listening to me.

T₇: Sounds like you have a hard time sorting me out from your mother.

As the process continues, the client connects early rageful feelings at mother with projecting mother onto the therapist and to current behavior. Alternate response strategies are then explored.

Supportive Approach

T₁: In what way did it feel like I didn't really care about you?

C₂: When I was talking about my mom being so angry you started taking notes...you weren't really listening...I'm just another case to you.

T₂: It sounds like it's very important to you that I care.

C₃: Yeah! When it seemed like you didn't, I just didn't know what to do. It felt like I couldn't go on. You're just interested in my money.

T₃: How can you know that I care about you?

C₄: I can't; it's clear you don't and never will.

T₄: It seems that you really want me to care but it's hard to trust that I do.

C₅: Yeah, nobody is trustworthy, everybody abandons me and now you are doing the same.

T₅: It feels like I'm abandoning you.

C₆: Yeah.

T₆: I am understanding how important being listened to is to you. It feels like abandonment when you don't feel listened to.

C₇: Yeah. It feels like I can't trust anybody.

T₇: That sounds lonely.

C₈: Yeah, now you know why it's so important to me.

Process continues in which the client feels supported, feelings are reflected, and the relationship is preserved. Through this process, the client is helped to build the skills necessary to respond to the sense of abandonment differently next time by talking about their needs and clarifying misunderstandings.

Expressive Approach

T₁: In what way did it feel like I didn't really care about you?

C₂: When I was talking about my mom being so angry you started taking notes...you weren't really listening...I'm just another case to you.

T₂: You have a lot of strong feelings about this.

C₃: You bet! I felt so mad...you're supposed to care and listen. I knew all along that you really didn't.

T₃: Is this a familiar feeling?

C₄: Yeah, my mom used to ignore me and wouldn't listen. I'd get so mad; it's like I wasn't even there.

T₄: It sounds like our relationship is very important to you?

C₅: No, it's not—I used to think it was, but now I know you don't care.

T₅: How did you feel when you thought I didn't care?

C₆: I couldn't stand it. I just had to do something.

T₆: So you cut on yourself.

C₇: Yeah, it makes me feel better.

T₇: It sounds like you were angry with me and you took it out on yourself.

C₈: Yeah, cause I know you really don't care to hear about me.

T₈: If you were to say to me now what you felt last week when you thought I wasn't listening, what would it be?

The process continues to help the client disclose feelings, stay focused on the current relationship, and learn how to have a stable relationship with the therapist.

What is the Psychoanalytic Approach to Treating BPD?

Although psychoanalytic theorists represent a school of thought within psychodynamic theories, their therapy focus differs enough to warrant separate reviews. According to these theorists, those with BPD experience early traumas or deficiencies in their environment that lead to a "*psychic deficit*."[82] For people with BPD to protect themselves from the painful awareness of the trauma experienced from their early caregiver, they inhibit their capacity to think about their own, as well as others' mental states. This inability to think about the thoughts, feelings, and actions of others and themselves leaves them with overwhelming emotions but no method for processing thoughts about these emotions.

Research indicates that those with BPD view themselves as hostile, labile and unstable.[83] Likewise, traditional psychoanalytic theorists maintain that people with BPD primarily defend against primitive aggressive impulses. Because they become easily overwhelmed by these and other emotions, helping them identify and cope with these emotions achieves the main treatment objective of producing basic personality change.

Pathological internalized object relations represent the greatest roadblock to effective BPD treatment. Instead of having hope that the therapist will be able to meet their perceived needs, clients' incapacity to tolerate primitive aggression leads to conflict-laden *transference*. These transference feelings result in a deep sense of distrust and fear of the therapist as an "attacker."

According to modern psychoanalytic theorists, a traditionally silent response to transference is not beneficial for people with BPD. The therapist needs to combine neutrality with a more active style of doing therapy due to the extreme tendency of those with BPD to misinterpret situations and comments.[82]

A review of psychoanalytic treatment strategies begins on page 32. Research results on the efficacy of using this approach to treat BPD are presented on pages 33 and 34.

psychic deficit— inadequately developed sense of self

The main focus of psychoanalytic therapy is to help the person with BPD identify and cope with the aggressive feelings that they work so hard to suppress.

object relations—"objects" are "others" who are the focus of love or affection. Thus, object relations are the present or past relationships with these love objects.

pathological internalized object relations—extremely dysfunctional relationships with the love objects which are now carried by the client as internal beliefs about relationships in general

transference—clients respond to therapists based on particular images of themselves, particular images or beliefs about therapists, and emotional reactions that connect the two

What are the Goals of Psychoanalytic Therapy?

Psychoanalysts target seven main goals for therapy.[82] These are to:

1. Help clients integrate their unidentified thoughts and feelings about themselves with their behaviors (reintegrate the split self).

2. Create an awareness and understanding of clients' object relations and how these affect current behavior.

3. Integrate these object relations (the positive and negative aspects, the abilities and inabilities, and the giving and the selfish tendencies) into clients' awareness to help them tolerate their own ambivalent feelings.

4. Limit the clients' acting out of negative impulses, particularly the self-harm impulses. Meeting this crucial goal requires explicit limit setting and the establishment of consequences for self-destructive behavior. Such consequences include interpretation, confrontation, suspending a session, enlisting the aid of others, and perhaps even termination of treatment.

5. Promote higher-level defensive functioning in which the clients' defense mechanisms become part of their awareness and are modified.

6. Work through the depression that has resulted from early trauma and abandonment.

7. Promote a sense of the clients' identity being separate from others.

How do I Treat BPD Using a Psychoanalytic Approach?

Like psychodynamic therapy, this theory holds that intrapsychic conflicts are the bases of behavior. There are two general techniques used in psychoanalytic therapy to help define the conflicts. These are maintenance of neutrality and *interpretation*.

The therapist must play an active role in repeatedly drawing the client's attention to the adverse consequences of self-destructive behaviors.[82]

interpretation—verbally giving meaning to the link between the client's unmet needs and current actions

Maintenance of Neutrality—The therapist must be able to express concern and objectivity in helping clients develop self understanding without making a personal investment in any one aspect of their behavior. By maintaining this neutrality, the therapist can interpret the needs clients present rather than gratify them. The neutral therapist can calm and support clients and consequently help them to order their internally chaotic world.

Interpretation—To use interpretation, the therapist hypothesizes as to what link exists between the conscious material the client presents and the client's unconscious motivations and needs. The therapist then communicates this hypothesis to the client.[72] Interpretations need to be made to an emotionally prepared client; therefore, techniques of *clarification* and *confrontation* often precede the use of interpretation.

Transference processes are the primary target for interpretation, and the analysis of transference reactions are considered the main vehicle of change. Having the therapist interpret transference helps clients integrate the separate aspects of their feelings and experiences. Interpretation also helps clients sort out reality from distortion in their reactions to the therapist. Additionally, by interpreting both positive and negative impulses toward the therapist, clients can integrate feelings of primitive aggression, which increases their ability to deal with ambivalence.

For the last several decades, practitioners have exercised caution regarding the use of psychoanalysis to treat those with BPD due to the propensity for *regression* into *psychotic transferences* and uncontrolled acting out. Additionally, some critics of the psychoanalytic approach believe that the emphasis on aggression may leave clients feeling even more critical of themselves for having the aggression. This may negate the possibility that the aggression may result from early environmental trauma and may lead clients to feel responsible for harm perpetrated on them by others.

How Effective is Psychoanalytic Therapy for Treating BPD?

A randomized, controlled study with severe BPD clients in a partial hospitalization treatment program compared psychoanalytic treatment to standard psychiatric care over the course of 18 months. The psychoanalytic treatment group

clarification—exploration of data that are vague or contradictory

confrontation—drawing the clients' attention to data that is discrepant or outside of their awareness

regression—reverting or retreating into an earlier, more childlike pattern of behavior

psychotic transference—grossly impaired reality testing regarding transference issues

The treatment example below demonstrates the psychoanalytical approach to the same initial client comment as that evaluated on page 30.

received therapy both individually and in a group setting. Psychoanalytic treatment produced significantly greater reductions in self mutilating behaviors, suicide attempts, length of inpatient treatment, anxiety, and depression, as well as improved global adjustment.[84]

Another outcome study focused on the administration of Kohut's self-psychology principals within the psychoanalytic school of thought.[85] The researchers found that following 12 months of individual therapy, there were reductions in impulsivity, affective instability, anger, medical office visits, self-harm behaviors, drug use, and suicidal behavior. However, instead of using a control group as comparison, this study utilized before-and-after survey measures.

The use of long-term treatment techniques is often neither feasible nor appropriate given that most people with BPD fail to complete even six months of treatment.[80]

Psychoanalytic Therapy Example (Client=C Therapist=T)

C_1: Last time we met I could tell you didn't really care about me, you were just seeing me for the money. I was so mad I went home and cut on my wrists. I couldn't help myself.

T_1: It seemed like I didn't care.

C_2: Yeah! I know you don't; you never did, you just pretended you did to get my money.

T_2: You sound very angry.

C_3: You bet I am. I can't stand it anymore. I may just go home and end it all because nobody cares.

T_3: It sounds like you are so angry at me you want to get back at me.

C_4: I hate you, you don't hurt like I do, you don't even know what it's like. Everybody leaves me and now you are leaving me too.

T_4: In what way am I leaving you?

C_5: You just don't care, you don't listen. You don't even care that I'm going to go home and kill myself.

T_5: I am noticing that you are angry with me and talking about killing yourself.

C_6: Yeah, I can't stand it anymore.

T_6: What can't you stand?

C_7: You leaving. I knew you would all along.

T_7: I notice that when you talk about leaving and killing yourself that then you say I am leaving.

C_8: I guess it's me who is leaving huh! It just hurts so bad I can't stand it.

T_8: And you feel so mad you want to kill me.

C_9: I didn't say that.

T_9: You are talking about me leaving.

C_{10}: Yeah, but I said I was going to kill myself.

T_{10}: How do you think that is related to killing me?

C_{11}: You said that, I didn't. Anyway, it seems easier to kill myself; it would still end the pain of wanting to kill you.

The dialog continues to explore the client's rage toward the therapist and self along with the connection to subsequent behaviors.

What is the Interpersonal Psychotherapy Approach to Treating BPD?

The basic premise of interpersonal psychotherapy is that people elicit behavior/communication from others based on a continuous interpersonal negotiation of getting their needs met. This theory assumes that current interpersonal interactions are reactions to earlier experiences in interpersonal relatedness.[73,86] Further, these interpersonal interactions shape one's self-view and become integrated into one's internal dialogue (self-talk). One interpersonal theorist describes all human experience as an internal dialogue or communication with other persons, whether imaginary or real; accordingly, a person's self has no existence apart from relationship with other persons.[87]

Interpersonal theorists maintain that people's rigid and narrow interactions with others cause dysfunctional behavior and communication. Selective attention, wherein people perceive only the information that agrees with and reinforces their particular view, continually reinforces these limited types of interactions. For example, if BPD sufferers seek nurturing and caring but believe that nobody can really meet their needs (based on earlier interpersonal relations), then they interact with others to make this belief come true. In order to make this belief come true, they may not recognize caring behaviors from others, or they may become easily angered and push the others away before their needs are met.

The above example closely relates to the interpersonal theory outlined in *System for Classifying Interpersonal Behavior* (SASB),[88] and the *Interpersonal Diagnosis and Treatment of Personality Disorders*.[89] This theory proposes that people respond to others based on dimensions of affiliation (hate to love) and control (a spectrum from submission to dominance). The pattern that characterizes people with BPD is that they are motivated to affiliate with and participate in control dimensions by "an intense fear of abandonment" and "a desire for protective nurturance," which starts as "friendly dependence" and then becomes "hostile control" when the caregiver "fails to deliver enough."[76] More specifically, this theory applies the interpersonal model to specific DSM

A review of interpersonal treatment strategies begins on page 37. Research results on the efficacy of using this approach to treat BPD are presented on page 38.

Within this model, psychiatric diagnoses and personality disorders can be made based on patterns of maladaptive interactions.[88]

criteria for BPD.[88] These theorists explain the link between the interpersonal model and BPD as follows:

1. The client internalizes abandonment from earlier relationships and behaves very recklessly with self-damaging impulsiveness.

2. Fear of abandonment comes from an early association with trauma and a feeling of self-blame for causing the abandonment. This blaming ("I'm a bad person.") results from punitive interactions with primary caregivers.

3. Internalization of neglect and its association with boredom and loneliness lead to feelings of emptiness.

4. Instability results from chaotic, early familial interactions that had serious consequences.

5. Those with BPD exhibit a famous anger set off by perceived abandonment that is intended to coerce the opposite of abandonment, namely nurturance.

6. Self-mutilation is a replay of early abuse from caregivers or an effort to appease an internalized attacker (negative internal message).

7. Identity disturbance stems from the internalization of early caregivers who would attack the person with BPD when there were signs of independence, self-definition, and/or happiness.

8. Self-sabotage amounts to self-protection from the internalized abusers.

9. Thought disorder or poor reality perception may result from negated reality testing in earlier interpersonal interactions.

According to interpersonal theorists, BPD clients interact with others in a highly rigid manner based on these nine concepts. This rigid, self-defeating style pushes others to responses that confirm the clients' beliefs. Those interacting with BPD sufferers feel they have a very narrow range of acceptable responses, a restriction that eventually leads to negative feelings and interactions. These negative interactions leave BPD sufferers baffled and angry since they perceive neither the role they play in the interaction nor their responsibility for the consequences.

How is BPD Treated Using the Interpersonal Therapy Approach?

Interpersonal psychotherapy treatment methods use a *collaborative* manner and focus on identifying self-defeating communication styles, clarifying reactions, and establishing alternatives to maladaptive behavior.

1. ***Identifying Self-Defeating Communication Styles***—Identifying these styles requires recognizing that clients will send the same rigid and self-defeating messages to the therapist that they send to others.

   To identify these styles through client-therapist interactions, therapists must recognize their own emotional responses and "pulls" in relation to clients. These emotional responses and "pulls" reflect what the therapist and others feel when interacting with the client. For example, if clients present themselves in a passive, demure, submissive manner, and the therapist has a "pull" (reaction) of wanting to take charge and be dominant, then these feelings can be used to help clients understand the impact their interactional style has on others. Clients can then begin to understand how they are actually creating the type of relationships they have.

2. ***Clarifying Reactions***—Once the therapist is aware of the "pulls" and "tugs" to respond in a certain manner to clients, the therapist needs to purposefully not respond that way. Instead, the therapist poses hypotheses to the client about the effects of such interactions. Additionally, one of the most powerful forms of therapeutic change is for therapists to respond to the client in a very genuine manner that clarifies their own "pulls" (reactions) to the client.

collaborative—therapist and client putting equal effort toward agreed-upon goals

---

The Main Goals of Interpersonal Therapy[89]

1. Facilitating a collaborative relationship with the client
2. Helping the client learn about their interaction patterns
3. Actively blocking the maladaptive interactional patterns during therapy sessions
4. Enabling and strengthening the will to change
5. Helping the client experience new interactional patterns

In addition to self-defeating communication styles, the therapist needs to help the client identify self-defeating behavior. Often self-destructive behavior follows interactions in which clients perceive that they will suffer "abandonment" or "being ignored." In a collaborative manner with clients, the therapist can help identify interpersonal interactions that precipitate self-injurious behaviors.

3. *Establishing Alternatives*—The goal during this phase is to help clients establish alternate patterns to previous maladaptive interpersonal patterns. These alternate patterns need to be more conscious, flexible, and choice-directed. In order to accomplish these goals, therapists and clients analyze the previous patterns of interaction that have produced undesirable results. Together, they discuss how the client has helped create these results and what alternate patterns exist. For example, if a client has a pattern of responding passively during an interaction and then later becoming angry and behaving in a self-harm manner, then the therapist will help the client engage in alternate, more active response patterns.

During the process of building new interaction patterns, therapists often use specific skill-building exercises. Such skill building includes assertiveness training, conflict resolution, and problem solving.

The treatment example on page 39 demonstrates how the interpersonal therapist might respond to the same initial comment by the client as used in the other examples.

How Effective is Interpersonal Therapy for Treating People with BPD?

The recently published interpersonal treatment approach outlined in the *System for Classifying Interpersonal Behavior* (SASB) lacks the supportive research to substantiate its effectiveness in treating BPD or other personality disorders. However, researchers utilized a more general type of interpersonal psychotherapy in treating BPD and compared it to other treatments, including cognitive behavioral therapy.[90] Results found cognitive behavioral therapy to be superior to interpersonal therapy over a 16-week period for people with BPD.

Interpersonal Therapy Example (Client=C Therapist=T)

C₁: Last time we met I could tell you didn't really care about me, you were just seeing me for the money. I was so mad I went home and cut on my wrists. I couldn't help myself.

T₁: You feel that I don't care.

C₂: I know you don't, you proved that last week!

T₂: Can you help me understand your anger?

C₃: What do you mean help you understand? You're supposed to care, you're my therapist.

T₃: You want me to care.

C₄: Damn right I do—but I know you don't really.

T₄: It is important to you that I care and yet when I am angrily accused of not caring, I feel the pull to be more distant rather than to come closer and be more caring.

C₅: So you don't care. I knew it all along.

T₅: I am saying that you are asking for my caring and closeness in a way that makes me feel pushed away rather than close.

C₆: So...I'm angry at you for not caring and you're saying it's my fault?

T₆: I'm wondering how we can resolve this in a way that you find out what you want, and we are closer rather than more distant.

C₇: What I want is to know if you care or not?

T₇: How can you find that out from me without pushing me away?

C₈: Well, I guess I could tell you how your taking notes last week made me feel and see if you meant it that way?

T₈: How would that be different than what you have already done?

C₉: Well, I guess I wouldn't just be accusing you, which you say makes you want to be more distant.

T₉: Yes. It sounds like this approach will be different for you.

C₁₀: Yeah, I'm used to just letting people know how angry I am.

T₁₀: Do you get the kind of response you want from them?

C₁₁: Well, they always prove me right!

T₁₁: They prove you right?

C₁₂: Yeah, I tell them I'm mad, and tell them why. Then, they can't handle it and go away.

T₁₂: So they become more distant instead of working out the problem with you.

C₁₃: Yeah, maybe it's kind of like what you were saying you feel...more distant.

The process continues with the therapist helping the client understand the impact they have on others and how that affects whether or not they get their needs met. This particular process focused on the needs for affiliation and how the client was engaging in patterns of communication that distanced others rather than engaged them. Further exploration would take place to help the client identify the interactional patterns that precipitate self-injurious behaviors.

The use of countertransference feeling in this approach is integral to the therapy process. However, therapists must be very careful to share their own thoughts and feelings only to the extent that they will be useful to their clients' understanding of their own communication patterns. Clients should not feel like they have to take care of the therapist.

A review of cognitive treatment strategies begins on page 42. Research results on the efficacy of using this approach to treat BPD are presented on page 45.

schemas—organized belief systems that attach meaning to events

Nine Common Maladaptive Schemas Characteristic of People with BPD[92]

1. **Abandonment/Loss**—"I'll be alone, no one will be there for me."
2. **Unlovability**—"No one would love me if they really got to know me."
3. **Dependence**—"I can't cope on my own, I need someone to rely on."
4. **Subjugation/Lack of Individuation**—"If I don't do what others want, they'll abandon me or attack me."
5. **Mistrust**—"People will hurt me, attack me, or take advantage of me. I must protect myself."
6. **Inadequate Self-Discipline**—"I can't control myself."
7. **Fear of Losing Emotional Control**—"I must control my emotions or something terrible will happen."
8. **Guilt/Punishment**—"I'm a bad person. I deserve to be punished."
9. **Emotional Deprivation**—"No one is ever there to meet my needs, to care for me."

What is the Cognitive Approach to Treating BPD?

This theory assumes that it is not an event in itself that leads to a particular consequence, but rather a person's belief about the event that gives it meaning and relates it to subsequent behavior. For example, high winds and dark clouds don't in themselves lead someone to run for cover. It is people's beliefs that these weather patterns result in tornados that lead them to seek shelter.

In the cognitive therapy of Personality Disorders, Beck relates that personality disorders are dysfunctions largely due to certain *schemas* that lead to biased judgments.[91] These dysfunctional schemas lead people to consistently create erroneous beliefs and interpretations of their own as well as other's actions which leads to dysfunctional emotion and behavior.

Cognitive Conceptualizations of BPD—Cognitive theorists view people with BPD as having extreme and poorly integrated views of relationships with early caregivers (similar to the object relations view). As a result, they hold extreme, unrealistic expectations regarding current interpersonal relationships. These expectations shape their behavioral and emotional responses and account for many BPD symptoms.

Beck proposes three basic assumptions underlying the perceptions and interpretations of a person with BPD.[91] These are:

1. *"The world is dangerous and malevolent"*— This perception leads to the conclusion that taking risks is dangerous. These risks include letting down one's guard, revealing a personal weakness, or being "out of control." Such beliefs lead to chronic feelings of tension, tiredness, suspicion, and guardedness.

2. *"I am powerless and vulnerable"*—This perception leads people with BPD to believe that they cannot deal with the dangerous and malevolent world they view. Clients typically resolve this dilemma by becoming dependent upon someone they see as capable of taking care of them. However, people

with BPD find this dependence unacceptable because they believe that they are inherently unlovable and unacceptable.

3. ***"I am inherently unacceptable"***—This belief keeps people with BPD from trusting others to maintain a relationship once that person "really gets to know me." Another common type of cognitive distortion in which people with BPD commonly engage involves overshadowing high-achieving activities with the belief that "I am a fake; someday, they will find me out."

The conflict between wanting to have someone to depend on and feeling inherently unacceptable causes the person with BPD to vacillate radically between autonomy and dependence, without being able to rely on either for emotional support.

An important goal of therapy is to help clients with BPD evaluate and modify their *dichotomous thinking*.[91] These extreme interpretations of events lead to extreme emotional responses and actions. With this type of thinking, there are no categories for intermediate perceptions. Therefore, the person with BPD may initially perceive others as reliable and completely trustworthy until the first time they fall short. At that point, they will be seen as completely untrustworthy. Dichotomous thinking precludes the idea that people may be trustworthy most of the time or in most situations.

dichotomous thinking— tendency to perceive and characterize situations, others' actions, and solutions as "black or white," "all or nothing," "good or bad," "trustworthy or deceitful," "successful or complete failures"

Because dichotomous thinking causes BPD clients to view themselves as either flawless or completely unacceptable, they see shortcomings in themselves as evidence that they are completely unacceptable as a person. Therefore, those with BPD feel that they must hide these shortcomings from others. Consequently, they must avoid intimacy and openness in a relationship for fear they will be "found out." By not getting the closeness and security from a relationship that they need, they will typically experience feelings of hopelessness. This self-reinforcing cycle is often quite resistant to change.

According to the cognitive approach, it is a greater challenge to change dysfunctional beliefs in people with personality disorders than in people with anxiety disorders due to the greater levels of extremes and rigid beliefs inherent in personality disorders.

One of the goals of cognitive therapy is to help clients test their underlying beliefs and modify them to bring about desired changes. This cognitive shift changes dysfunction-causing beliefs into an anxiety state necessary for change and, ultimately, into more functional belief systems.

How is BPD Treated Using the Cognitive Approach?

Beck outlines eight intervention strategies for treating the person with BPD using a cognitive theoretical approach.[91] These are:

Building a collaborative relationship is often a slow process even though it is an important treatment factor.

1. ***Develop trust in the relationship and use a collaborative strategy***—Establishing the therapist/client relationship in and of itself challenges most of the assumptions held by those with BPD. A trusting relationship can most easily be established when the therapist openly acknowledges how difficult it must be for clients to trust based on the number of painful experiences they have had in the past. Then, the therapist must behave in a consistently trustworthy manner by only making promises that can be kept and by carefully defining the relationship so that clients know what to expect.

2. ***Choose an initial focus of therapy with the client that will lead to some immediately felt progress***—Behavioral goals can often be useful at this point in therapy because they take the focus off of the difficulties involved in maintaining trust and intimacy.

3. ***Reduce or eliminate dichotomous thinking early in therapy***—As the main contributor to extreme actions, mood swings, and dilemmas faced by those with BPD, reducing dichotomous thinking should reduce symptom intensity as well as help modify underlying assumptions and provide alternate resolutions to many dilemmas. To change dichotomous thinking, the therapist should point out examples to the client as they occur and then discuss whether thinking in terms of a continua would lead to more realistic and adaptive responses.

Transference reactions are a very rich source of material for uncovering dysfunctional thoughts and assumptions.

4. ***Deal with the transference issues in the session***—Transference can best be understood in cognitive terms as clients responding to the therapist based on generalized beliefs and expectations they have about relationships, rather than according to how the therapist behaves as an individual.

When strong emotional reactions occur that appear to be related to transference reactions, the therapist must deal with them promptly. Cognitive treatment practitioners suggest the following process:

- Develop a clear understanding of what the client is thinking and feeling.

- Resolve misunderstandings and misconceptions clearly and explicitly.

- Convey that the client will not be rejected or attacked because of emotional reactions.

5. ***Address the client's fear of change directly by examining the risks involved in trying things a new way***—One perception common among people with BPD that is based on fear of change is that therapy will be over as soon as the problems are overcome. If this is the case, the therapist needs to clarify that termination of therapy will be a collaborative decision as are other decisions about therapy.

6. ***Help clients increase control over their emotions by acknowledging their emotions and modeling appropriate ways to respond to them***—The therapist can help clients look critically at their thoughts in a problem situation and develop alternate coping strategies. These strategies involve learning adaptive ways to express emotions. While developing these more active and assertive responses, the therapist should proceed slowly and should continue to talk about the risks in changing behavior patterns. For example, many people with BPD believe expressing a feeling such as anger will lead to immediate rejection or attack by the recipient.

7. ***Improve impulse control by acknowledging and dealing with the client's initial response to changing behavior, "Why should I?"***—Most people with BPD have been told numerous times that they should better control themselves. As a result, they will likely oppose behavior change.

Strategies for Treating BPD Using Cognitive Therapy[91]

1. Focus on developing trust in the relationship and a collaborative strategy.

2. Choose an initial focus of therapy with the client that will lead to some immediately felt progress.

3. Reduce or eliminate dichotomous thinking early in therapy.

4. Deal with the transference issues in the session.

5. Address the client's fear of change directly by examining the risks involved in trying things a new way.

6. Help the client increase control over their emotions by acknowledging their emotions and modeling appropriate ways to respond to them.

7. Improve impulse control by acknowledging and dealing with the client's initial response to changing behavior, "Why should I?"

8. Strengthen the client's sense of identity.

In choosing whether to act on an impulse, the client will not necessarily need to behave in ways that they may later regret.

Therapists need to convey to clients that they are not trying to enforce societal norms, but that they are helping them to choose whether to act on an impulse or not. The process of developing impulse control involves:

- Identification of impulses

- Exploration of the pros and cons of controlling impulses

- Development of alternatives to responding to impulses

- Examination of the expectations and fears that block promising alternatives

- Providing skills training or coaching necessary for the client to utilize new alternatives

Additionally, the therapist needs to discuss what the impulse behavior means to the client as well as the motivation for performing that behavior. For example, self-mutilation acts may come from a desire to punish others, punish oneself, obtain relief from guilt, or as a distraction from more aversive thoughts and feelings. Knowing the motivation behind the behavior can help in developing alternate coping strategies.

Feedback by the therapist must be provided in an honest and realistic manner so that it does not appear insincere.

8. ***Strengthen the client's sense of identity***—Help clients identify their positive characteristics and accomplishments and provide them with positive feedback regarding their resourceful decisions and effective coping. In addition, have them evaluate their own actions realistically as a means of strengthening their own ability to provide positive self reinforcement. The client/therapist relationship presents the single most important opportunity for providing positive feedback; the therapist can provide positive feedback to the client by recognizing difficult risks the client takes in therapy.

How Effective is Cognitive Therapy for Treating BPD?

There are few controlled outcome studies assessing the efficacy of cognitive therapy with BPD. However, one study completed by the National Institute of Mental Health found cognitive behavioral therapy to be superior to interpersonal therapy over a 16-week period for treating people with BPD.[90]

The following treatment example demonstrates how the cognitive therapist might respond to the same initial comment as used in previous examples.

Cognitive Therapy Example   (Client = C   Therapist = T)

C_1: **Last time we met, I could tell you didn't really care about me, you were just seeing me for the money. I was so mad I went home and cut on my wrists, I couldn't help myself.**

T_1: It sounds like you were very angry.

C_2: You bet I was. I knew you didn't care about me all along.

T_2: What were you feeling when you decided to cut on yourself?

C_3: I already told you, I was very angry with you.

T_3: When you were feeling angry, what were you thinking?

C_4: I was thinking that life was hopeless, nobody would ever care about me. Not even you.

T_4: You were thinking that nobody cares about you and never will in the future?

C_5: Kinda like that.

T_5: Well I can see why you felt hopeless. I believe I would too if nobody cared about me, and nobody ever would in the future. That sounds pretty lonely. What kept you from killing yourself?

C_6: Well it wasn't bad enough to kill myself.

T_6: What do you mean it wasn't "bad enough"?

C_7: Well, I was really mad at you. I guess I didn't really think "nobody" cares. If nobody cared, I think I would kill myself.

T_7: There are some people in your life that care about you?

C_8: Yeah, I guess.

T_8: How do you know when someone cares about you.

C_9: Well they listen to me, and talk to me, and help me.

T_9: Who do you know who listens to you and talks to you?

C_{10}: Well, my friend Trudy does.

T_{10}: How well does she do? Is she pretty good at being able to listen to you most of the time?

C_{11}: Yes, she's always there when I need her. I can always count on her.

T_{11}: That's pretty amazing that she is always there. Most friends are able to be there a lot of the time, but not all of the time.

C_{12}: Well yes, I guess she's not there all the time, but most of the time.

By admitting that a relationship that is significant is not "perfect," the therapist continues the process by bringing the discussion back to the current relationship with the therapist. The goal is to help the client acknowledge feelings of wanting the therapist to "always" be attentive and "perfect," but let the client know the therapist cares and will be there but not "always" or "perfectly." The technique is to have the client identify the ability to have a "non-perfect" caring relationship in a less threatening way and then transfer that understanding to the current therapeutic relationship.

A review of dialectical behavior treatment strategies begins on page 48. Research results on the efficacy of using this approach to treat BPD are presented on page 53.

dialectical—systematic reasoning processes where a person tries to resolve contradictory ideas

emotional dysregulation— emotional imbalance or poor emotional control

blocking—disruption or inhibition of thought processes

What is the Dialectical Behavior Therapy (DBT) Approach to Treating BPD?

DBT is an approach originally developed by Linehan to treat suicidal behaviors.[92-95] This approach, which has been expanded to treat people with BPD, focuses on the inherent tension between often-opposing forces. For example, on one hand, the therapist needs to initiate change in the client and, on the other hand, the therapist must demonstrate acceptance of the client as they are "in the moment." Both forces are critical to the BPD treatment and highlight the *dialectical* bases of treatment.

DBT is based on a long term treatment model that views BPD in a biosocial model. The theory proposes that those with BPD have a biologic predisposition toward *emotional dysregulation* coupled with an emotionally invalidating environment. These forces interact to produce the dysfunction seen in BPD. DBT focuses on three sets of opposing forces that clarify primary BPD conflicts:

1. *Emotional Vulnerability vs. Self-Invalidation*—The **emotional vulnerability syndrome** refers to the poor ability that many people with BPD have in regulating their emotions. They are extremely sensitive to even low-level emotional stimuli. They tend to react quickly and have more intense responses to emotions than non-BPD individuals. Additionally, they return more slowly to their own emotional baseline, consequently they will often go to great lengths to avoid emotions by using denial, avoidance, *blocking*, and shutting down. When unable to avoid emotion, they intensely overreact with extreme emotional displays or engage in various dysfunctional escape behaviors such as substance abuse and/or other self-harm behaviors. Some research indicates that this type of emotional sensitivity is constitutional in nature.[96]

   The **self-invalidation syndrome** describes the discounting of personal feelings. People with BPD were often raised in environments where feelings were negated or not attended to and thus they failed to learn how to accept, label, or control their own feelings.[97] The vulnerability to extreme emotions coupled with the lack of validation for these emotions leads the person to various responses including feeling guilty, overwhelmed, and afraid that their emotions are uncontrollable.

2. ***Unrelenting Crises vs. Inhibited Grieving***— Those with BPD often live in a perpetual state of crisis, while desperately trying to avoid or inhibit feelings of grief that result from the crises. ***Unrelenting crisis*** refers to the repeated emotional reactivity experienced by the person with BPD. Intense emotional reactions increase distress because they interfere with the ability to plan behaviors, as well as the ability to think clearly and problem solve. Because the ability to tolerate one's own emotions is so low, those with BPD often engage in counterproductive escape behaviors such as drinking, spending money, engaging in unprotected sex, and leaving situations, which creates more losses and crises.

   Inhibited grieving syndrome refers to a pattern of recurrent loss as a result of the many crises created by unpredictable behavior and emotional stress. Crisis of any kind involves loss, whether it be concrete such as the loss of a job, a significant other, a predictable environment, or abstract such as the loss of acceptance by someone. The loss is not experienced and grieved due to the poor ability to deal with emotions. This creates a perpetual system of *bereavement overload.* [98]

3. ***Active Passivity vs. Apparent Competence***—*Active passivity* refers to the tendency of those with BPD to demand that their difficulties be resolved by others in their environment. The passivity stems from a sense of hopelessness because the individual has learned few coping responses and cannot avoid extreme negative emotions. This hopelessness often leads to interpersonal dependency marked by emotional clinging and demanding behaviors.

unrelenting crisis—the individual does not return to an emotional baseline before the next crisis hits

bereavement overload— overwhelming number of feelings related to grief and loss

active passivity—the tendency to approach problems in a passive and helpless manner

apparent competency syndrome—tendency to appear deceptively competent

The *apparent competency syndrome* highlights how those with BPD may mask their true feelings or adopt the attitude of others, even in painful situations. This often results in clients appearing very competent in a particular situation, while later displaying extreme negative emotions to the bewilderment of those around them. Thus, the person may behave appropriately and competently in one situation, which gives observers the false impression that they are able to act competently across many situations.

How is BPD Treated Using the Dialectical Behavior Therapy Approach?

Four primary stages of treatment comprise DBT; Overall Stabilization, Helping Clients Heal the Effects of Trauma, Addressing Residual Problems that Interfere with Achieving Personal Goals, and Helping Clients Resolve Feelings of Incompleteness. Within these stages clients focus on seven main dialectical forces, and therapists use six primary types of treatment strategies.[6,93,94]

Stages of Treatment

Stage 1: Overall Stabilization— The goals of this stage include the following:

- Decreasing life threatening behaviors such as suicide, unprotected sex and substance abuse.

- Increasing connections to helping individuals such as family members, therapist, and supportive friends.

- Reinforcing stability, capabilities, and control of action, in order to achieve goals. These include increasing skills in interpersonal effectiveness, distress tolerance skills such as feeling and respecting emotional discomfort, and increasing objective thinking skills including observing, describing, taking a non-judgemental stance, and being effective with one thing in the moment.

DBT Behavioral Targets

1. Decrease suicide behaviors
2. Decrease behaviors that interfere with therapy
3. Decrease behaviors that interfere with quality of life, such as substance abuse, homelessness, joblessness, or poor relationship abilities
4. Increase coping skills of emotional regulation, distress tolerance, and interpersonal skills
5. Decrease post-traumatic stress responses through accepting and changing current patterns between thoughts, feelings, and behaviors
6. Enhance self-respect
7. Focus on achieving individual client goals

Stage 2: Helping Client's Heal the Effects of Trauma in Their Lives— Healing the effects of trauma includes focus on the following:

- Understanding early trauma such as neglect and physical and sexual assaults and reducing counterproductive avoidance behaviors.

- Increasing productive connections to people, places and activities such as supportive family and friends and work.

Stage 3: Addressing Residual Problems that Interfere with Achieving Personal Goals— This is accomplished through focusing on patterns of behavior that increase self-respect and self-trust.

Stage 4: Helping Client's Resolve Feelings of Incompleteness and Increasing Their Capacity for Sustained Joy— This stage primarily focuses on setting additional personal goals, expanding awareness, and spiritual fulfillment.

Areas of Focus for Clients

The seven main opposing forces or dialectical areas of focus for clients include the following:

1. **Self acceptance and problem acceptance versus improving one's effectiveness and problem solving—** This involves acceptance of one's own strengths, weaknesses and problems in order to decrease guilt, shame and distress, balanced with actively engaging in skill building and problem solving in order to initiate change.

2. **Tolerating Emotions versus Regulating and Controlling Emotions—** Clients increase their ability to tolerate uncomfortable and painful emotions in order to reduce counterproductive avoidance behaviors such as self-mutilation, shutting off feelings, or leaving situations. Additionally, clients learn to regulate and control overwhelming emotions through the use of specific distraction or self-soothing strategies.

Because of their high levels of emotional discomfort, those with BPD tend to be very self-focused.

3. *Seeking Help and Depending on Others versus Independence and Self-Efficacy*— Clients learn to find a balance between needing and relying upon others for support and help versus believing in their own independent abilities and personally taking care of problems or dilemmas.

4. *Focusing on Others versus Focusing on One's Self*— Clients increase their ability to attend to other peoples thoughts and feelings, as well as their own. Focusing on and giving to other people helps them improve relationships and feel better about themselves.

5. *Participating Effectively versus Attending and Watching*— Clients identify ways to control or change a situation through effective participation, while also balancing times of observing and watching how events unfold. This develops reflection and impulse control skills in order to increase planned behavior.

6. *Revealing One's Self to Others versus Retaining Privacy*— Clients decide which personal thoughts and feelings to share with others in order to build relationships versus thought and feelings they keep private in order to increase self-respect and healing.

Finding a balance between trust and suspicion encourages more reflective and moderate interactions with others.

7. *Trusting Others versus Suspecting Others*— Instead of vacillating between extremes of total trust or total suspicion of others, clients identify specific characteristics or circumstances with others that can or cannot be trusted.

Treatment Strategies for Therapists

Treatment approaches for DBT involve the use of six specific strategies.[6,93,94] These are:

wise mind—the part of the person that pays attention and attaches meaning to all that is happening around them

1. *Dialectic Strategies*—Dialectic strategies include the use of stories, myths and paradoxes focused on helping the client balance cognitive and emotional extremes as well as use their *wise mind.*

The therapist focuses on six primary opposing forces to help clients find interpersonal, emotional, and cognitive balance. The main dialectical strategies during treatment sessions include:

- Alternating acceptance and change strategies to encourage a collaborative working alliance with the client.

- Balancing nurturing and accepting responses with demands for the client to actively change or help herself.

- Focusing on the client's capabilities, as well as on personal limitations and deficits.

- Modeling critical and observational thinking by focusing on the client's viewpoint, as well as other perspectives or missing information.

- Describing and encouraging flexibility and change on a developmental level, while acknowledging the client's need for stability.

- Synthesizing thoughts and feelings that appear opposite in order to help client's identify the middle path inherent in all aspects of life.

2. *Focusing on Commitment*—Therapists ask the client to commit to small, initial steps of change before eventually asking for larger commitments to change. Likewise, they approach commitment by asking for more than the client will give, and then reducing the request until the client commits. These strategies focus on getting the client to commit to changes that reinforce adaptive, non-suicidal behavior and extinguish maladaptive and suicidal behaviors.

   The therapist must convey that the change-making process consists of taking small steps toward a larger goal rather than trying to change too quickly.

3. *Validation Strategies*—These strategies focus on accepting, empathizing with, and reflecting on the client's behaviors and feelings in light of **present** circumstances. This process involves:

   - Discovering and helping the client understand how their current behavior protects them from something painful.

   The therapy relationship is best for challenging the assumption that, "I am inherently unacceptable." The therapist challenges this assumption through honestly appreciating the client for who they are and helping them to perceive themselves as acceptable.

- Perpetually putting forth the belief that the client wants to improve. This position requires the therapist to acknowledge how feelings of shame, fear, and anger may inhibit improvement.

4. ***Problem-Solving Strategies***—Problem-solving strategies focus on change. Once the therapist and client identify a problem behavior, skills training can be used to increase coping capabilities; cognitive strategies can be used to modify beliefs, rules, and expectancies; and *contingency* management can be used to increase incentives for adaptive coping.

5. ***Reciprocal Communication and Irreverent Communication Strategies***—These strategies seek to interweave communications of warmth, acceptance and closeness with a matter-of-fact approach and confrontation. The therapist uses self-disclosure to model coping skills and encourage self-disclosure by the client. Irreverent communication strategies balance therapist responses of warmth and acceptance with the introduction of more offbeat responses to maladaptive behaviors. These offbeat responses may help "unbalance" the client creating a shift that promotes acceptance of a new viewpoint. If used carefully, this strategy can facilitate problem-solving without the risk that excessive attention may reinforce suicidal or escape behaviors.

6. ***Case Management Strategies***—The therapist can use these strategies to balance the techniques of providing environmental interventions in situations where immediate outcomes are very important, with consultant-to-the-patient strategies that encourage the client to act on their own behalf. Additionally, the therapist can use self-supervision/consultation to balance the tension between caring for one's self and caring for the client.

contingency—an agreement between the therapist and client regarding specific behaviors that will be followed by specific reinforcers or punishers

The therapist must neither reinforce suicidal behavior through excessive attention nor ignore these behaviors to the point that the client escalates them to a life-threatening level.

The treatment example on the following page demonstrates how the DBT therapist might help validate the client's feelings and support the development of alternate behaviors. Compare this example with the previous treatment examples; all respond to the same initial comment by the client.

How Effective is Dialectical Behavior Therapy in Treating BPD?

In the only randomized, controlled study of psychotherapy effectiveness in treating BPD, Linehan and colleagues found DBT (using stages 1 and 2), to be superior to "treatment as usual in the community" as measured by fewer parasuicidal behaviors, fewer inpatient hospitalizations, lower attrition rates, and less medically severe parasuicides following one year of therapy.[99,100] There was no follow up assessment to measure the sustained effects of treatment. Other non-controlled studies found DBT superior to "treatment as usual in the community" in terms of clients reporting significantly less anger, greater social adjustment, better work performance, less anxious rumination, and feeling less severely disturbed following one year of therapy.[101,102] Adaption of short term DBT to inpatient settings have not proven effective.[103]

In these efficacy studies, clients who were randomly assigned to the "treatment as usual in the community" group received treatment from various community professionals, most of whom reported that they practiced behavioral or cognitive-behavioral therapy.

Dialectical Behavior Therapy Treatment Example (Client=C Therapist=T)

C_1: **Last time we met I could tell you didn't really care about me, you were just seeing me for the money. I was so mad I went home and cut on my wrists, I couldn't help myself.**

T_1: What made it seem like I didn't care?

C_2: You started taking notes when I was telling you how angry I was with my mother.

T_2: When I wrote some notes that meant that I didn't care about you?

C_3: Right, that you weren't really listening to me.

T_3: I can understand how my looking away from you in order to write a note seemed as if I wasn't listening. I am sorry that it came across that way and you felt discounted.

C_4: Yeh, well!

T_4: I'm wondering when you became aware of feeling angry?

C_5: Right away. I just didn't say anything.

T_5: So when you went home and cut on yourself that was your way of stopping the angry feelings?

C_6: Yes, and it worked for a while.

T_6: I'm wondering how you can honor your angry feelings without cutting on yourself.

C_7: Honor my anger?

T_7: Right. Your feelings are important.

C_8: Well, that seems like a joke, but I guess I could tell you when I'm angry.

T_8: How will that help you know that I'm listening and I care about you?

C_9: I guess if you quit taking notes or something.

T_9: We could figure out another method for remembering important things you say.

C_{10}: Hum, well I guess we could come up with something. Honoring my anger! That sure is different. My anger doesn't seem so unbearable when I look at it like that.

The dialog continues with focus on helping the client tolerate uncomfortable angry feelings, as well as problem solve regarding note taking.

What is the Cognitive Analytic Therapy Approach to Treating BPD?

Cognitive Analytic Therapy, a newly developed brief integrative treatment model, focuses on learned patterns of relating to others. This developmental model emphasizes early childhood experiences and learned relationship roles that are the focus of treatment. Clients learn to recognize their repertoire of *reciprocal roles* so that they may decide how to revise their behavior to be more functional and adaptive. Preliminary research on the effectiveness of this approach is promising.[104-108]

reciprocal roles— thoughts and actions directed toward eliciting or predicting a particular response from others..

What is the Relapse Prevention Therapy Approach to Treating BPD?

In relapse prevention therapy, the overall aim is to teach the client how to achieve a *balanced lifestyle* and to prevent unhealthy habit patterns by anticipating and coping with relapse.[109] By acquiring new skills and cognitive strategies, the client can regulate new behaviors with higher mental processes including awareness and responsible decision-making. However, this process requires the client to take an active position toward mastering new skills. This is problematic for people with BPD until their characteristic passive stance has been sufficiently moderated. In this model, therapists view addictive behavior as an acquired habit pattern rather than as a disease.

balanced lifestyle—a lifestyle in which the client has control of their behavior and chooses behaviors that are generally moderate

One of the main assumptions of this theory is that factors associated with the initial development of an addictive behavior may be independent of factors associated with changing that behavior. For example, the initial development of alcoholism may be the result of a genetic aberration or of an unbalanced metabolic system. Based on this etiology, some would expect a change in drinking behavior to be brought about only through a biomedical intervention. Instead, relapse prevention therapy strives to help clients master the skills necessary to live the life they desire.

Relapse prevention is a theoretical model for treating people who struggle with addictions. Since people with BPD often have one or more addictions or compulsive behaviors based on immediate gratification, the components of relapse prevention represent important considerations for treatment.

To better understand addiction, both therapist and patient should know that addictive actions are usually followed by some form of immediate gratification (e.g., a high state of pleasure or tension reduction), which increases the desire to repeat the behavior. However, these behaviors are unhealthy to the extent that they lead to delayed but negative social, health, and/or self-esteem consequences.

The relapse prevention model supports the view that uncontrollable addictive behaviors are cyclical in nature. The cycle works like this:

1. It starts with loss of control (indulgence).
2. Loss of control is followed by internal or external pressures to stop the behavior.
3. These pressures are then followed by a decision to abstain from the behavior (absolute control/ restraint).
4. Abstinence is usually followed by a violation of this control (a slip).
5. A slip leads to beliefs about one's self, such as "I have no willpower," "I can't change," or "I'm meant to be this way."
6. These beliefs complete the cycle as they lead to a loss of control.

The goal of relapse prevention therapy is to help clients be aware of their behavior, choose skills appropriate to the situation, and follow a behavior course that is midway between restraint and indulgence.

The relapse prevention model for treating addiction requires active client participation in changing behavior. The model proposes three stages of change:

1. ***Motivation and Commitment to Change*—**
   Motivation to change may come from an individual desire, an awareness of long-term negative consequences, failure to derive the desired beneficial effects, or confrontation from others. Once the therapist determines the client's motivation, the two need to discuss the commitment to change and the client's sense of timing and lifestyle. If the commitment to change is not carefully considered, an impulsive attempt to change based on the motivation may fail. This failure makes a client reluctant to recommit to the change process.

Cycle of Addictive Behavior

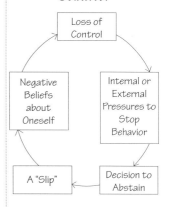

Though this is a learning model the assumption is not that the person is solely responsible for their addictions. Rather, addictions are viewed as a result of behavioral reinforcement which is usually not in the awareness of the individual.

The Relapse Prevention Model of Change

Motivation and Commitment to Change

Implementation of Change

Maintenance of Change

2. ***Implementation of Change***—This stage includes utilizing behavioral, cognitive, and lifestyle interventions targeted toward changing from a maladaptive pattern of responding to a more purposeful response pattern.

3. ***Maintenance of Change***—This stage is the most difficult of all and needs the most attention. Maintenance begins the moment abstinence or control begins. Because this is the stage in which clients will be faced with multiple temptations, they need planned strategies to cope with these urges. Old, problematic habits must be "unlearned," and new behaviors must be acquired. Most *mistakes* are likely to occur during this stage as clients gradually learn new replacement behaviors. These mistakes subside as clients master new response patterns. These mistakes are considered *lapses*, while a total reversal to the old behavior patterns is considered a *relapse*.

Therapists give lapses and relapses a framework, allowing clients to view them as a way to learn what is needed to make new behavior patterns work. In these instances, it may be better to term the slip as a *prolapse* because this term suggests working toward an overall beneficial outcome.

mistakes—recurrences of behaviors being "unlearned" and framed as mistakes to be learned from

lapse—mistakes that occur when clients give in to urges with "old" behavior patterns

relapse—a total reversal to "old" behavior patterns

prolapse—a way of viewing relapses as a slide or fall forward that allows the client to learn from the relapse

Since social pressure accounts for 20 percent of relapses, the clients' social interactions may influence them to engage in undesired behaviors. These interactions need to be brought to light and planned for. Many of these situations are considered high risk; however, when effective cognitive or behavioral coping responses can be made, the probability of relapse decreases significantly.[109]

Because clients' negative emotional states (e.g., anger, sadness, frustration, and feelings of abandonment) have been involved in 35 percent of relapses, the therapist should assess with the client the main sources of negative (unpleasant) emotional reactions.[109] These sources include:

- Various interpersonal interactions
- Negative self-image
- Learned beliefs that cause distressful emotional reactions

How is BPD Treated Using the Relapse Prevention Model?

1. **Take a Collaborative Approach**—Work with clients from the beginning to help them understand that the behavior is something they do rather than something they are. In order for therapy to be collaborative, clients should be involved in selecting their own combination of techniques. Plan small but incremental successes, rather than applying a wide range of techniques that overwhelm the client.

2. **Identify Antecedents to the Lapse**—These antecedents can be related to situational, environmental, or cognitive factors. Family history and prior learning can also be associated with the lapse. Often, analyzing the chain of behaviors and cognitions that led to the lapse helps identify points of intervention. Important cognitive antecedents are:

   • Rationalizations utilized
   • Denial of circumstances or feelings
   • Choice points within the chain of events

3. **Use Cognitive Strategies**—These strategies provide the client with thought processes regarding change (e.g., "I am changing learned habits rather than personality characteristics," "The change process is a learning process," "Change is a journey."). High-risk situations are similar to dangerous driving conditions in which drivers must exercise extra caution and skill to prevent an accident. These strategies include:

   • Using imagery of a high-risk situation accompanied by imagery of employing alternate coping responses, called *relapse rehearsal*.

   • Teaching clients *detachment* from their urges. This approach teaches clients to monitor their urges or desires and to watch those desires come and go or wax and wane from the

---

Treating BPD with Relapse Prevention Therapy

1. Take a collaborative approach
2. Identify antecedents to the lapse
3. Use cognitive reframing
4. Conduct skills training
5. Implement lifestyle interventions
6. Create a lifestyle balance

---

relapse rehearsal—a technique that uses imagery of a high-risk situation accompanied by imagery of employing alternate coping responses

detachment—monitoring urges by observing them come and go without acting on them

---

The knowledge gained from using these skill-building exercises gives the client more choices and better flexibility in responding to future interpersonal situations.

systematic desensitization—progressively more intense exposure to the feared situation

behavioral rehearsal—during the therapy session, the therapist helps the client rehearse responses to feared situations

substitute indulgences—alternative indulgences with a more positive outcome such as having a massage, eating a gourmet meal, exercising, going to dinner with a friend, spending leisure time in the park, or going to a movie

position of an observer. Watching urges come and go without engaging in the undesired behavior helps the urges to eventually subside.

4. ***Incorporate Skills Training***—Skills training includes teaching both cognitive and behavioral responses to deal with high-risk situations. This approach includes first identifying high-risk situations through monitoring ongoing behavior or describing past relapse episodes. When clients encounter high-risk situations, they can be instructed to "slow down and stop" before proceeding any further or to "reconsider the road ahead" or to consult a "road map" for alternate "routes." Then, alternate coping strategies can be used.

Coping strategies for these high-risk situations include problem-solving strategies and conflict management. For those clients whose coping strategies are blocked by fear or anxiety, appropriate anxiety-reduction procedures can be used (e.g., relaxation, *systematic desensitization*.) General skills training can involve direct instruction, modeling, *behavioral rehearsal*, coaching, and feedback from the therapist.

5. ***Develop Lifestyle Interventions***—Building relaxation and exercise into the client's lifestyle will help strengthen the overall coping capacity and reduce the stress level of the client. This can reduce the frequency and intensity of the urges toward the old behavior. Another form of lifestyle intervention is to teach the client to utilize *substitute indulgences*, or activities to provide the immediate form of self-gratification previously experienced by the undesired behavior.

6. ***Create Lifestyle Balance***—Creating a balance in lifestyle between activities perceived as "shoulds," "have-tos," or "hassles" and those perceived as "pleasurable," "self-fulfilling," or "wants." When their lifestyle is weighted down with "hassles," clients often associate these hassles with a perception of self-deprivation which leads to a desire for indulgence and

gratification. Once clients learn to recognize and control these contingencies, they should:

- Set their own standards
- Monitor their own performance
- Reinforce themselves appropriately

How Effective is Relapse Prevention Therapy in Treating BPD?

At this time, there are no controlled outcome studies assessing the effectiveness of using relapse prevention as treatment specifically for BPD.

The following treatment example highlights how the therapist focuses on the maladaptive behavior as "an old habit," taps into the client's motivation for change, and focuses on the decision-making process. Compare this example with the previous treatment examples; all respond to the same initial comment by the client.

Relapse Prevention Therapy Treatment Example (Client = C Therapist = T)

C_1: **Last time we met I could tell you didn't really care about me, you were just seeing me for the money. I was so mad I went home and cut on my wrists, I couldn't help myself.**

T_1: You sound pretty angry.

C_2: You bet I am. I knew you didn't care about me all along.

T_2: How did feeling angry at me lead you to cut on yourself?

C_3: Well I was mad at you. I didn't know what to do. I just couldn't stand it anymore.

T_3: Instead of telling me you were angry with me you went home and hurt yourself. How did you decide to do that?

C_4: Well I didn't know how mad I was until I left here. Then, I didn't know what to do with my anger, so I did what I'm used to doing.

T_4: You decided to cut on yourself.

C_5: Yeah.

T_5: How did you decide to do that instead of something else?

C_6: Well, it feels better. Remember, I told you before; it takes the anger away.

T_6: Remember in the past when you decided you wanted to change that old response pattern? What led you to that decision?

C_7: Well, it seemed like I just hurt myself and then it didn't really fix things. I'd like to learn how to fix things instead of hurting myself.

T_7: Next time you are angry with me, let's try to think of something else you could try instead of hurting yourself.

C_8: Well, when I feel really mad like that I could call you and tell you I'm mad and see if it's true.

T_8: That's a very good idea. What will you do If I'm not available right then when you call?

C_9: Well, I can go over to my friend Trudy's house and talk to her. Being with her, I won't cut on myself. If she's not there, I can go walk around the park.

T_9: I'm glad you have some choices for dealing with that old habit next time. It sounds like feeling angry at me is a high-risk situation for you.

The dialog process continues to help the client identify high-risk situations, connect thoughts and feelings that have led to the old habit in the past, and develop alternate thoughts, feelings, and behaviors for the future.

Five Constants of Individual BPD Therapy

1. Creating a stable treatment environment

2. Providing active interventions and responses

3. Establishing a connection between the client's actions and present feelings

4. Taking the gratification out of performing self-destructive behaviors

5. Paying careful attention to countertransference feelings

Therapists treating BPD clients should use ongoing supervision to review the client's progress and to discuss countertransference feelings that may adversely direct the therapy.

countertransference—therapists' emotions that are triggered by something the client said or did

How are Various Individual Therapy Approaches Similar?

Although many differences exist between individual psychotherapy approaches, researchers agree on five basic components as necessary for treating people with BPD.[110] These are:

1. ***Creating a Stable Treatment Environment***—Given the capacity of people with BPD to regress into psychotic perceptions, therapists must clarify and maintain the consistency of roles, schedule, fees, and other boundary issues. Some research indicates that clients perceive this structure as supportive, and it introduces organization into their chaotic lives.[111]

2. ***Providing Active Interventions and Responses***—The therapist must be alert and active in identifying, confronting, and directing the client's behavior. This activity diminishes the amount of transference distortions and provides a framework of therapist supportiveness.

3. ***Establishing a Connection Between the Client's Actions and Present Feelings***—This connection helps clients identify feelings and motives behind their behavior and often includes setting limits on behaviors that threaten the safety of the client, therapist, or continuation of therapy.

4. ***Taking the Gratification Out of Performing Self-Destructive Behaviors***—The therapist must consistently identify, or help clients identify, the adverse consequences of their self-destructive acts.

5. ***Paying Careful Attention to Countertransference Feelings***—BPD clients have the capacity to evoke feelings of anger and helplessness in the therapist because therapists perceive them as more dominant and hostile than other clients.[112] Clients can also evoke sustained patterns of *countertransference* feelings (e.g., the need to be idealized, needed, omnipotent, or submissive). If acted upon, these feelings can be detrimental to the therapeutic relationship and need to be monitored.

How Can Group Psychotherapy Help People with BPD?

Many therapists report that they find group psychotherapy to be the treatment of choice for people with BPD, and many clients value their group therapy experience over individual therapy. A number of therapists believe individual therapy in conjunction with group therapy is the most effective treatment.[113]

Most theoretical approaches to treating BPD focus on the nature of interpersonal relationships as the cause and the key to maintenance of the disorder. Therefore, group therapy (which offers multiple interpersonal relationships in a controlled setting) gives the person with BPD important opportunities to make the changes necessary for more productive functioning.

Group therapy offers a variety of useful approaches that are particularly advantageous for the person with BPD. These include:

1. *Reality Testing*—Regular feedback from group members is one of the most powerful advantages of group therapy. Clients often accept difficult feedback more easily from peers than from an authority figure (the therapist). The continuous feedback from group members helps decrease interpersonal distortions and intense expressions of primitive fears and needs.

2. *Viewing How the Client Relates to Others*—Yalom notes that in group therapy, clients will recreate their familial relationships and dynamics (as well as other outside relationships) with members in the group.[101] This provides extremely useful information about the client's outside relationships for therapists to use according to their theoretical orientation.

3. *Reducing Transference Reactions*—These reactions, which are often intense and take a long time to process during individual therapy, are significantly reduced in group therapy. This reduction is due to the increased number of people that provide

This review focuses on the rationale and benefits for using group therapy conducted by a trained group psychotherapist. Specific interventions and techniques are **not** addressed. The information presented is written for those already experienced in conducting group treatment or those who are planning to refer a client to group therapy.

Useful Approaches Afforded by Group Therapy for Treating BPD

1. Reality testing
2. Viewing how the client relates to others
3. Reducing transference reactions
4. Healing
5. Identification
6. Stimulation
7. Peer pressure
8. Changing behavior

reality testing and the increased number of recipients of transference reactions.

4. *Healing*—Group therapy offers a healing aspect to people with BPD through the process of being taken seriously and respected by the other group members.

5. *Identification*—During group therapy, people with BPD often watch how the therapist interacts with other group members and internalize some of these behaviors to increase their own coping and interpersonal skills. Additionally, this same *identification* process may take place with other group members. Hopefully, the client chooses to identify (internalize) the positive coping skills of other group members rather than the negative ones.

6. *Stimulation*—More Schizoid-like (withdrawn) BPD clients may benefit from the stimulation of group interaction.

7. *Peer Pressure*—Peer pressure can help set limits for members with poor control over impulsive behaviors.

8. *Changing Behavior*—Group therapy provides an avenue for members to be part of a group and to increase their ability to be intimate with others. Group dynamics often center around the methods, including self-mutilation, members use to avoid intimacy. Group therapy is an avenue for changing these patterns.

How Effective is Group Psychotherapy for Treating BPD?

Several controlled studies have been done assessing the effectiveness of group therapy for people with BPD.[78,92,114-116] The results of these studies indicate decreases in parasuicidal behavior, improved work status, and improvement in severe BPD symptoms. Research conducted on Yalom's curative factors indicates that the most helpful group factors for people with BPD are *Universality* and *Existential Factors*.[113,117]

What are the Biological Influences that May Cause BPD?

Some research indicates that BPD may be of a genetic, neurological, and/or biologic origin. Theoretical approaches based on this research promote the use of *psychopharmacological* treatments for those with BPD. This review focuses on genetic as well as neurological and/or biological indications of BPD and addresses medication treatment strategies and efficacy.

psychopharmacological— medications that affect thought processes, mood, and behavior

Genetic Indications

Genetic indications come from research indicating that BPD is about five times more common among first-degree, biological relatives of those with the disorder than those in the general population.[3] This finding could either be due to genetic links or could indicate the impact of environmental influences on the disorder. Further genetic information comes from research conducted in the 1980s that found parents of those with BPD to have a low incidence of schizophrenia and a high incidence of affective disorder.[118]

Also during the 1980s, researchers found that biological markers of sleep latency and Rapid Eye Movement measurements were similar among those with BPD and those with Major Depressive Disorder. However, these findings have subsequently been refuted,[119] and new auditory biological markers (auditory 300) now link BPD mor closely to Schizophrenia.

Neurological and/or Biological Indications

Throughout BPD literature, four prominent clusters of BPD symptoms emerge with different underlying biological substrates.[120-123] These clusters are:

1. Affective Instability
2. Depression
3. Transient Psychoticism
4. Impulsive Aggressive Behavior

adrenergic—a neuronal pathway in the adrenal gland that produces adrenaline also known as epinephrine

cholinergic—neurons and neural pathways that release the neurotransmitter, acetylcholine, which is involved in stimulating sweat glands and fibers to skeletal muscles

decompensation—a failure of one's defense mechanisms leading to an exacerbation of BPD symptoms

dopaminergic—neural pathways in which the neurotransmitter dopamine (which appears to inhibit motor control systems and limbic activity) is involved

neurotransmitter—chemical agents that affect behavior, mood, and feelings

limbic—associated with autonomic functions and certain aspects of emotions and behavior

serotonergic—neurons and neural pathways that release the neurotransmitter serotonin

visiospatial—environmental spatial relationships that are processed visually

Affective Instability—This cluster of symptoms is related to abnormalities in the brain's *adrenergic* and *cholinergic* systems. Symptoms include labile affect, irritability including inappropriate and intense outbursts of anger, instability of mood, low mood or dysphoria, and stress related *decompensation*.

Depression—This cluster of symptoms is related to abnormalities in the brain's *adrenergic* and *cholinergic* systems. It includes symptoms of depressed mood, loss of interest in life's activities and pleasures, insomnia or hypersomnia, poor attention and concentration, and recurrent suicidal ideation.

Transient Psychoticism—Abnormalities in central *dopaminergic* systems may underlie transient psychotic experiences. The *neurotransmitter* dopamine appears to be important in motor control systems, *limbic* systems, and Schizophrenia. Symptoms of transient stress related psychoticism include referential thinking, derealization or depersonalization, paranoia, distortion of reality, and magical thinking.

Impulsive Aggressive Behavior—Abnormalities in central nervous system *serotonergic* functioning appear to underlie impulsive aggressive behaviors, particularly suicide attempts.[122-127] Additionally, high levels of the cerebrospinal fluid concentration of monoamine metabolites 5-hydoxyindoleacetic acid (5-HIAA), appears to protect against impulsive or suicidal behavior.[127] Symptoms include suicide and parasuicidal behavior, self-mutilation, food or alcohol binges, promiscuity, assaultive behavior, and antisocial acts.

Further support for a biological component to BPD comes from research indicating brain abnormalities in those with BPD. Specifically, 40% of BPD subjects showed non-localized brain dysfunction in the form of abnormal diffuse, slow activity, noted from recorded electroencephalograms (EEG's).[128]

Cognitive mechanisms also appear to be involved in BPD. Some research suggests biological differences between BPD and normals of impaired *visiospatial* processing that requires learning and recall of novel, complex information. Additional deficits appear in visiospatial discrimination, speed, and fluency. These findings do not appear to be related to depression, psychomotor deficits, or attention problems. Additionally, Rorschach studies have found deviant communication patterns, an inability to maintain or shift cognitive sets, and odd reasoning.[125] These results suggest patchy, underdeveloped cognitive functioning among those with BPD that is, at this point, still of uncertain origin.

How Can Pharmacological Treatments Help People with BPD?

Although there are numerous psychopharmacological interventions for BPD, researchers have found no single medication superior to another for the broad spectrum symptoms of BPD. Deciding which psychopharmacological agent to prescribe depends on the presenting symptoms.[122,123,129] Due to the suicide potential of the person with BPD, the prescribing physician must carefully consider the lethality of the medication and the number of pills given in a single prescription.

The therapist needs to be aware of the important dynamics that can take place when a client is using psychotropic medications.[130] Plan to address these dynamics during therapy sessions:

- Medication may encourage the client to engage in magical thinking about a quick passive cure which reduces the motivation for psychotherapy.

- The recommendation for medication may be perceived by clients as a personal assault based on a perception that psychotherapy is more socially acceptable and more useful to "healthier" clients.

- Clients and physicians who believe in the purely biological underpinnings of mental illness (e.g., a chemical imbalance) view the effectiveness of the medications as treating the neurophysiological deficiencies and thus view psychotherapy as excessive or unnecessary.

- Psychopharmacotherapy can effect psychotherapy because the medications prescribed often improve central nervous system functions such as attention and concentration. Verbal abilities, memory, and motor capacities are often increased as well. Greater functioning in these areas allows clients to be more cognitively and verbally accessible to psychotherapy.

Prescribing Medication Can:

- Reduce the motivation for psychotherapy

- Be perceived as a negative indicator of the client's condition

- Increase cognitive functioning which can enhance psychotherapy

65

Comparative Matrix of Psychopharmacological Treatments

Target Symptoms	Class of Drug/ Drug	Typical Dosage	Side Effects
++ impulsive/ aggressive ++ affective instability ++ depression	**Monoamine Oxidase Inhibitors (MAOIs)** (Antidepressant drugs that operate by blocking the metabolism of dopamine, epinephrine, and norepinephrine). Tranylcypromine (Parnate) Phenelzine (Nardil)	mgs./day 20-60 30-75	Common side effects are dry mouth, blurred vision, drowsiness, urinary hesitance, constipation, light-headedness, and hypertension. Less common side effects are restlessness, insomnia, anorexia, nightmares, decreased sexual potency, tiredness, flushing, skin rash, and hallucinations. **These drugs may be lethal in overdose** and pose a risk of hypertensive crisis due to tyramine food reaction. Foods to avoid while on MAOIs are cheese, beer, red wine, sherry, liquors, yeast/protein products (such as brewers yeast and yeast in some packet soups), fava or broad bean pods, smoked fish, beef, or chicken liver, figs, sauerkraut, and stewed whole bananas.
++ impulsive/aggressive ++ affective instability ++ depression	**Selective Serotonin Reuptake Inhibitors (SSRI's)** (group of medications that selectively block the re-uptake of the neurotransmitter serotonin) Citalopram (Celexa) Fluvoxamine (Luvox) Fluoxetine (Prozac)[131] Paroxetine (Paxil) Sertraline (Zoloft)	mgs./day 20-60 200-300 20-60 40-60 50-200	**Side effects may include:** Sexual dysfunction, decreased appetite, nausea, fatigue, daytime sedation, nervousness, restlessness, anxiety, agitation, respiratory complaints, headache, dry mouth, tremors, diarrhea or constipation, insomnia, anorexia or increased weight gain, frequent urination, dizziness, and sweating. **Except for fluoxetine,** rapid discontinuation of SSRIs is commonly associated with symptoms of withdrawal, which persist for 1-2 weeks.Typical SSRI withdrawal symptoms include dizziness, headache, tingling, "electric-shock" sensations, and flu-like symptoms.
++ Depression - -these are contraindicated for impulsive/ aggressive	**Tricyclic Antidepressants (TCAs)** (group of antidepressant drugs that act by reducing the neuronal uptake of acetycholine which is part of skeletal muscle system, autonomic nervous system, and parasympathetic nervous system functioning): - Amytriptyline - Imipramine - Desipramine Doxepin Nortriptyline	mgs./day 100-200 100-200 100-200 70-150 50-100	**Common side effects** are dry mouth, constipation, urinary hesitance, blurred vision, confusion, and memory disturbance. Less common side effects are drowsiness, weight gain, hypotension (diminished tension or tone in muscle, or abnormally low blood pressure). **These drugs may be lethal in overdose** and may precipitate dyscontrol with increased suicidality, assaultiveness, and psychoticism. Schizotypal features may predict poor response.

Legend: ++ strong treatment effect; + modest treatment effect; -- negative effect on symptoms.
See page 64 for description of target symptoms

Comparative Matrix of Psychopharmacological Treatments

Target Symptoms	Class of Drug/ Drug	Typical Dosage	Side Effects
++ impulsive /aggressive ++ psychoticism	**Neuroleptics** (antipsychotic medications): Chlorpromazine Clozapine[132,133] Fluphenazine Haloperidol Loxapin Molindone Mesoridazine Olanzapine Perphanazine Pimozide Quetiapine Risperidone Thiothixene Thioridazine Trifluoperazine Ziprasidone	<u>mgs./day</u> 50-150 25-400 5-10 1-10 50-80 25-100 50-300 5-10 4-16 5-10 100-600 2-4 2-20 100-600 5-10 20-60	**Common side effects** are blurred vision, urinary retention, dry mouth, constipation, decreased sweating, and memory difficulty. Less common side effects are acute dyskinesia (muscle spasms), Akathisia (extreme restlessness), Parkinsonism (tremor, very flat affect, poor sensory-motor coordination, exhaustion, and loss of ability to initiate action), Neuroleptic Malignant Syndrome (hyperthermia, muscle rigidity, flushing, unstable blood pressure, tachycardia), and Tardive Dyskinesia (irreversible Parkinsonism).
++ impulsive/aggressive + affective instability	**Lithium Carbonate** (a salt that changes the composition of body fluids) has been found effective at the end of six weeks.	Based on individual response	**Common side effects** are nausea, cramps, diarrhea, hand tremor, muscle weakness, fatigue, insomnia, thirst, headache, and decreased concentration. Less common side effects include weight gain, hypothyroidism, polydipsia (drinking of extreme amounts of water), and skin rashes.
++ impulsive/aggressive + affective instability	**Anticonvulsants** Carbamazepine Valproic Acid Divalproex	<u>mgs./day</u> 200-1200 750-1500 750-1500	**Common side effects** are itching, hives, rashes hypotension, hypertension, congestive heart failure, urinary retention, dizziness, fatigue, incoordination, visual disturbance, speech disturbance, depression, and gastrointestinal distress. This drug may cause lethal bone marrow suppression and thus must be used with complete blood count monitoring (CBC) **For Valproic acid and Divalproex:** Pancreatitis is rare but serious & occurs early in treatment. Hepatitis most common in children, usually within first 6 months of treatment
++ dissociative symptoms	**Opiate Antagonists** Naltrexone[134]	<u>mgs./day</u> 75-300	**Common side effects** include nausea, insomnia, headache, anxiety, fatigue, dizziness, weight loss, and joint and muscle pain.
- - contraindicated for impulsive/aggressive due to increase in behavioral dyscontrol including suicide attempts and other behavioral outbursts	**Benzodiazepines** (sedative agents) Alprazolam Lorazepam	<u>mgs./day</u> 1-6 1-6	**Common side effects** are drowsiness, lightheadedness, fatigue, weakness, loss of coordination, less common side effects include confusion, hallucinations, depression, amnesia, paradoxical stimulation of hyperactivity, insomnia, rage, and anxiety.

Legend: ++ strong treatment effect; + modest treatment effect; -- negative effect on symptoms.
See page 64 for description of target symptoms

How Effective is a Pharmacological Approach in Treating BPD?

Research has found no psychopharmacological agent to be superior to another for the broad spectrum of BPD symptoms.[129,131] Clinicians have found these medications most effective for acute symptoms. Medications generally show limited efficacy when used for maintenance.[122,123,129]

Therapy Notes
From the Desk of Pat Owen

Terminated individual therapy with J.W. who successfully utilized two months of medication treatment. J. responded well in individual therapy to the structured environment of regular sessions and clear rules regarding his suicidal gestures. No cutting or suicidal ideation for last 3 months. J. is currently able to identify his feelings and connect his feelings to his actions. His actions are more planned and purposeful rather than impulsive (e.g., planned a discussion with Alex to convey his anger at her, rather than sever the relationship). No evidence of derealization, paranoia, or referential thinking. Still uses alcohol 3-4 times a week, but no longer uses Cannabis or amphetamines. Pattern of idealization and devaluation has improved with J. demonstrating more moderate reactions to others. I recommended starting group therapy in order to maintain his progress and improve his social functioning.

Glossary

A

adrenergic—a neuronal pathway in the adrenal gland that produces adrenaline also known as epinephrine

affect—emotion; feeling; mood

atypical depression—out of the ordinary depressive symptoms such as periods of elated mood, or periods of interest and activity

B

balanced lifestyle—a lifestyle in which the client has control of their behavior and chooses behaviors that are generally moderate

behavioral rehearsal—during the therapy session, the therapist helps the client rehearse responses to feared situations

bereavement overload—overwhelming number of feelings related to grief and loss

blocking—disruption or inhibition of thought processes

C

cholinergic—neurons and neural pathways that release the neurotransmitter, acetylcholine, which is involved in stimulating sweat glands and fibers to skeletal muscles

clarification—exploration of data that are vague or contradictory

cluster B personality disorders—the group of personality disorders which involves dramatic, emotional, or erratic behavior

collaborative—therapist and client putting in equal effort toward agreed upon goals

compulsive—feeling compelled to act against one's wishes

confrontation—drawing the clients' attention to data that is discrepant or outside of their awareness

convergent validity—when test results positively correlate with other instruments measuring the same variable

countertransference—therapist's emotions that are triggered by something the client said or did

D

decompensation—a failure of one's defense mechanisms leading to an exacerbation of BPD symptoms

denial—the process whereby the client responds to an event as if it is not or has not happened

delusion—a belief that is maintained despite much evidence or argument to the contrary

depersonalization—a sense that one has lost contact with one's own personal reality, e.g., a client might relate that, "My body feels strange, like it's not my own"

derealization—a sense that one has lost contact with external reality

detachment—monitoring urges and observing urges come and go without acting on them

devaluation—the process whereby the client undervalues the abilities and/or intentions of others

dialectical—systematic reasoning processes where a person tries to resolve contradictory ideas

dichotomous thinking—a tendency to perceive and characterize situations, others' actions, and solutions as "black or white," "all or nothing," "good or bad," "trustworthy or deceitful," "successful or complete failures"

discriminate validity—an instrument's ability to discriminate a particular disorder from other disorders

dissociation—an abnormal psychological state in which one's perception of oneself and/or one's environment is altered significantly

dissociative ego states—attitudes and emotions that produce anxiety become separated from the rest of the person's personality and function independently

dopaminergic—neural pathways in which the neurotransmitter dopamine (which appears to inhibit motor control systems and limbic activity) is involved

DSM-IV—The Diagnostic and Statistical Manual of Mental Disorders-Fourth Edition

dysphoria—mild chronic depression

E

emotional dysregulation—emotional imbalance or poor emotional control

environmental structuring—setting guidelines, limits, and rules for the process of therapy

existential factors—social aloneness, self responsibility, coming to terms with mortality

H

hallucinations—hearing or seeing things others do not

hyperphagia—pathologically excessive talking

I

idealization—the process whereby the client sees another person as only "good" or "perfect"

identification—process whereby the client internalizes aspects of important others

impulsive—acting without first thinking about the action

interpretation—verbally giving meaning to the link between the client's unmet needs and current actions

interrater reliability—degree that different raters agree on a diagnosis based on the use of the instrument

intrapsychic—within a person

L

labile affect—marked and rapid mood shifts

lapse—mistakes that occur when clients give in to urges with "old" behavior patterns

limbic—associated with autonomic functions and certain aspects of emotions and behavior

M

maladaptive behavior patterns—patterns of behavior likely to produce so much psychic distress that therapy is necessary

micropsychotic—minor psychotic symptoms such as derealization, depersonalization, paranoia, and referential thinking

mild formal thought disorder—disturbances in speech, communication, and/or thinking

mistakes—recurrences of behaviors being "unlearned" and framed as mistakes to be learned from

MMPI—Minnesota Multiphasic Personality Inventory, a widely used instrument assessing personality and symptoms of distress

N

naturalistic studies—observation and documentation of therapy in the natural setting

neurosis—non-physiological disorder characterized by high levels of anxiety but no impairment in reality testing

neurotransmitter—chemical agents that affect behavior, mood, and feelings

O

object relations—"objects" are "others" who are the focus of love or affection; thus, object relations are the present or past relationships with these love objects

P

paranoia—having unfounded suspicions and beliefs that one is being followed, plotted against, persecuted, etc.

pathological internalized object relations—extremely dysfunctional relationships with the love objects which are now carried by the client as internal beliefs about relationships in general

projective identification—the process whereby the client behaves toward others in such a manner that elicits the very behavior that will confirm their own underlying beliefs

projective measure of personality (as measured by the Rorschach)—the stimuli or inkblots are assumed to be neutral; they were created randomly and have no specific shape nor function; shapes, movement, and other elements of the pictures that clients see in the blots are a product of the client's own experiences and perceptual orientation projected on the cards

prolapse—a way of viewing relapses as a slide or fall forward that allows the client to learn from the relapse

psychic deficit—inadequately developed sense of self

psychopharmacological—medications that affect thought processes, mood, and behavior

psychosis—grossly impaired reality testing with such symptoms as delusions, hallucinations, referential thinking, and paranoia

psychotic transference—grossly impaired reality testing regarding transference issues

R

reciprocal roles— thoughts and actions directed toward eliciting or predicting a particular response from others..

referential thinking—believing others' actions or external events are specifically related to you when they are not

regression—reverting or retreating into an earlier, more childlike pattern of behavior

relapse—a total reversal to "old" behavior patterns

relapse rehearsal—a technique that uses imagery of a high-risk situation accompanied by imagery of employing alternate coping responses

S

schemas—organized belief systems that attach meaning to events

sensitivity ratio—percent of cases correctly identified by the instrument

serotonergic—neurons and neural pathways that release the neurotransmitter serotonin

specificity ratio—percent of non-cases correctly identified by the instrument

splitting—the division of self and others into "all good" or "all bad" categories, which results in sudden reversals of feelings and conceptualizations about one's self and others

substitute indulgences—alternative indulgences with a more positive outcome such as having a massage, eating a gourmet meal, exercising, going to dinner with a friend, spending leisure time in the park, or going to a movie

systematic desensitization—progressively more intense exposure to the feared situation

T

taxonomy—classification system

transference—the client responds to the therapist based on a particular image of themselves, a particular image or belief about the therapist, and an emotional reaction that connects the two

transient psychotic experiences—psychotic symptoms are reality impairment symptoms that include delusions, hallucinations, personalization, referential thinking, and paranoia; transient psychotic symptoms indicates that these symptoms tend to occur during times of severe stress and abate after the stress ceases

U

universality—the sense of not being alone in one's struggles

unrelenting crisis—the individual does not return to an emotional baseline before the next crisis hits

V

validity—degree that the instrument measures what it reports to measure

visiospatial—environmental spatial relationships that are processed visually

W

WAIS-R—Wechsler Adult Intelligence Scale-Revised

Bibliography

1.   Kroll, Carey, Sines, and Rothe. (1982). Are there borderlines in Britain? A cross-validation of U.S. findings. Archives of General Psychiatry, 39, 60-63.

2.   Ronningstam, E. & Gunderson, J. (1991). Differentiating borderline personality disorder from narcissistic personality disorder. Journal of Personality disorders. 5(3), 225-232.

3.   American Psychiatric Association. (1994). Diagnostic and statistical manual of mental disorders. (4th ed.) Washington, D.C.: American Psychiatric Association.

4.   American Psychiatric Association. (1987). Diagnostic and statistical manual of mental disorders (3rd ed., rev. ed.). Washington, DC: Author.

5.   Swartz, M., Blazer, D., George, L, & Winfield, I. (1990). Estimating the prevalence of borderline personality disorder in the community. Journal of Personality Disorders. 4(3), 257-272.

6.   Bellack, A.S., & Hersen, M. (1990). Handbook of comparative treatment for adult Disorders. New York: John Wiley & Sons.

7.   Stone, M.H., Hurt, S. W., & Stone, K. (1987). Long-Term follow-up of borderline inpatients meeting DSM-III criteria: I. Global outcome. Journal of Personality Disorders. 1 (4), 291-298.

8.   Trull, T.J., Useda, J.D., Conforti, K., & Doan, BT. (1997). Borderline personality disorder features in nonclinical young adults: Two-year outcome. Journal of Abnormal Psychology. 106, (2), 307-314.

9.   Paris, Joel (1990). Completed suicide in borderline personality disorder. Psychiatric Annals. 20(1), 19-21.

10.   Stone, M., Hurt, S. W., & Stone (1987). The PI 500: Long-term follow-up of borderline inpatients meeting DSM-III criteria. I. Global outcome. Journal of Personality Disorders, 1(4), 291-298.

11.   Siegel, M.A. , Landes, A., Foster, C.D. (Eds.) (1993). Health-A concern for every american. Wylie, TX: Information Plus.

12.   Solof, P.H. Lynch, K.G., Kelly, T.M., Malone, K.M. & Mann, J.J. (2000). Characteristic of suicide attempts of patients with major depressive episode and borderline personality disorder: A comparative study. American Journal of Psychiatry, 157, 601-608.

13.   Plakun, E. M. (1991). Prediciton of outcome in borderline personality disorder. Journal of Personality Disorders, 5(2), 93-101.

14.   Paris, J., Brown, R. & Nowlis, D. (1987). Long-term follow-up of borderline patients in a general hospital. Comprehensive Psychiatry, 28, 530-535.

15.   Zanarini, M. C., Gunderson, J. G., Frankenburg, F. R., Chauncey, D. L., & Glutting, J. H. (1991). The face validity of the DSM-III and DSM-III-R criteria sets for borderline personality disorder. American Journal of Psychiatry. 148(7), 870-874.

16.   Clarkin, J. F., Widiger, T. A., Frances, A., Hurt, S. W., & Gilmore, M. (1983). Prototypic typology and the borderline personality disorder. Journal of Abnormal Psychology, 93, 263-275.

17.   Widiger, T. A., Sanderson, C., & Warner, L. (1986). The MMPI, prototypal typology, and borderline personality disorder. Journal of Personality Assessment, 51(2), 228-242.

18.   Blais, M.S., Hilsenroth, M.J., & Fowler, J.C. (1999). Diagnostic efficiency and hierarchical functioning of the DSM-IV borderline personaltiy disorder criteria. Journal of Nervous and Mental Disease, 187 (3), 167-173.

19.   Snyder, S., Pitts, W. M., & Pokorny, A. D. (1986). Selected behavioral features of patients with borderline personality traits. Suicide and Life Threatening Behavior. 16(1), 28-39.

20.   Hurt, S. W. & Clarkin, J. F. (1990). Borderline personality disorder: Prototypic typology and the development of treatment manuals. Psychiatric Annals. 20(1): 13-18.

21.   Blais, M.A., Hilsenroth, M.J., & Castlebury, F.D. (1997). Content validity of the DSM-IV borderline and narcissistic personality disorder criteria sets. Comprehensive Psychiatry, 38 (1), 31-37.

22.   Kernberg, O. (1975). Borderline conditions and pathological narcissism. New York: Aronson.

23.   Wilkinson-Ryan, R., & Westen, D. (2000). Identity disturbance in borderline personality disorder: An emperical investigation. American Journal of Psychiatry, 157, 528-541.

24.   Fiqueroa, E.F., Silk, K.R. Huth, A. & Lohr, N.E. (1997). History of childhood sexual abuse and general psychopathology. Comprehensive Psychiatry, 38 (1), 23-30.

25.   Links, P.s., Helelgrave, R., & van Reekum, R. (1999). Impulsivity: Core aspect of borderline personality disorder. Journal of Personality Disorders, 13 (1), 1-9.

26.   Stein, K.F. (1996). Affect instability in adults with a borderline personality disorder. Archives of Psychiatric Nursing, 10 (1), 32-40.

27.   Dougherty, D.M., Bjork, J.M., Huckabee, H.C., Moeller, F.G., & Swann, A.C. (1999). Laboratory measures of aggression and impulsivity in women with borderline personality disorder. Psychiatry Research, 85 (3), 315-326,

28.   Levine, D., Marziali, E. & Hood, J. (1997). Emotion processing in borderline personality disorders. Journal of Nervous and Mental Disease, 185 (4), 240-246.

29.   Kemperman, I., Russ, M.J., Shearin, E. (1997). Self-injurious behavior and mood regulation in borderline patients. Journal of Personality Disorders, 11 (2), 146-157.

30.   Zanarini, M. C. , Gunderson, J. G., Frankenburg, F. R, & Chauncey, D. L. (1989). The revised diagnostic interview for borderlines: Discriminating BPD from other Axis II disorders. Journal of Personality Disorders. 3(1), 10-18.

31.   Spitzer, R. L., Williams, J. B. W., & Gibbon, M. (1987). Structured clinical Interview for DSMIII-R. New York: New York State Psychiatric Institute.

32.   Fogelson, D. L., Nuechterlein, K. H., Asarnow, F.R., Subotnik, K.L., and Talovic, S.A. (1991). Interrater reliability of the structured clinical interview for DSM-III-R, Axis II: Schizophrenia spectrum and affective spectrum disorders. Psychiatry Research. 39(1), 55-63.

33.   Morey, L.C. (1991). Personality Assessment Inventory. Odessa Fl: Psychological Assessment Resources, or San Antonio, TX: The Psychological Corporation.

34.   Bell, P., Virginia, J., Pate, J.L., & Brown, R.C. (1997). Assessment of borderline personality disorder using the MMPI-2 and the Personality Assessment Inventory. Assessment, 4 (2), 131-139.

35.   Leichsenring, F. (1999). Development and first results of the Borderline Personality Inventory: A self-report instrument for assessing borderline personality organization. Journal of Personality Assessment, 73 (1), 45-63.

36.   Marziali, E., Muroe-Blum, H., & McCleary, L. (1999). The Objective Behavioral Index: A measure of assessing treatment response of patients with severe personality disorders. Journal of Nervous & Mental Disorders, 187 (5), 290-295.

37. Sansone, R.A., Wiederman, M.W., & Sansone, L.A. (1998). The Self-Harm Inventory (SHI): Development of a scale for identifying self-destructive behaviors and borderline personality disorder. Journal of Clinical Psychology, 54 (7), 973-983.

38. Beck, A.T. (1991). Beck Scale for Suicide Ideation (BSS). San Antonio, TX: The Psychological Corporation.

39. Cull, J.G., & Gill, W.S. (1988). Suicide Probability Scale. Los Angeles, CA: Western Psychological Services.

40. Hathaway, S. R., Butcher, J.N., & McKinley, J. C. (1989). Minnesota Multiphasic Personality Inventory-2. Minneapolis, MN: University of Minnesota Press.

41. Graham, J. R. (1990). MMPI-2: Assessing personality and psychopathology. New York: Oxford University Press.

42. Greene, R. L. (1991). The MMPI-2/MMPI: an interpretive manual. Boston: Allyn and Bacon.

43. Zalewski, C. & Archer, R. P. (1991). Assessment of borderline personality disorder. Journal of Nervous and Mental Diseases. 179(6), 338-345.

44. Gartner, J. Hurt, S. W., Gartner, A. (1989). Psychological test signs of borderline personality disorder: A review of the empirical literature. Journal of Personality Assessment, 53(3), 423-441.

45. Kaufman, A. S. (1990). Assessing adolescent and adult intelligence. Boston: Allyn & Bacon, Inc.

46. Rapaport, D., Gill, M. M., & Schafer, F. (1945). Diagnostic psychological testing. (Vol. 1). Chicago: Year Book.

47. Exner. J.E. (1993). The Rorschach: A comprehensive system; volume 1:basic foundations. Somerset, New Jersey: John Wiley and Sons.

48. Millon, T. (1987). Millon clinical multi-axial inventory-II. Minneapolis: National Computer Systems.

49. Fine, M.A. & Sansone, R.A. (1990). Dilemmas in the management of suicidal behavior in individuals with Borderline Personality Disorder. American Journal of Psychotherapy. XLIV (2), 160-169.

50. Kernberg, O. (1993) . Suicidal behavior in borderline patients: Diagnosis and psychotherapeutic considerations. American Journal of Psychotherapy, 47(2), 245-254.

51. Brodsky, B.S., Malone, K.M., Ellis, S.P., Dulit, R.A., & Mann, J.J. (1997). Characteristics of borderline personality disorder associated with suicidal behavior. American Journal of Psychiatry, 154 (12), 1715-1719

52. Borges, G., Walters, E.E., & Kessler, R.C. (2000). Associations of substance use, abuse, and dependence with subsequent suicidal behavior. American Journal of Epidemiology, 151, 781-789.

53. Kotsaftis, A. & Neale, J. M. (1993). Schizotypal personality disorder I: The clinical syndrome. Clinical Psychology Review (Vol 13), 451-472.

54. Gunderson, J.G., Zanarini, M.C., & Kisiel, C.L. (1991). Borderline personality disorder: A review of data on DSM-III-R descriptions. Journal of Personality Disorders. 5(4), 340-352.

55. Zanarini, M.C., Frankenburg, F.R., Dubo, E.D., Sickel, A.E., Trikha, A., Levin, A. & Reynolds, V. (1998). Axis 1 comorbidity of borderline personality disorder. American Journal of Psychiatry, 155 (12), 1733-1739.

56.   Fenton, W.S. & McGlashan, T.H. (1990). Long-term residential care: Treatment of choice for refractory character disorder? Psychiatric Annals. 20:1, 45-49.

57.   Koenigsberg, H. (1984). Indications for hospitalization in the treatment of borderline patients. Psychiatric Quarterly. 56, 247-258.

58.   Miller, L.J. (1989). Inpatient management of borderline personality disorder: A review and update. Journal of Personality Disorders, 3(2), 122-134.

59.   Barley, W. D., Thorward, S. R., Logue, M. A., McCready, K. F., Muller, J. P., Plakun, E. M., and Callahan, T. (1983). Characteristics of borderline personality disorder admissions to private psychiatric hospitals. The Psychiatric Hospital, 17(4), 195-199.

60.   Hull, J.W., Yeomans, F., Clarkin, J. Li, C., & Goodman, G. (1996). Factors associated with multiple hospitalizations of patients with borderline personality disorder. Psychiatric Services, 47 (6), 638-641.

61.   Perry, J. C., Herman, J. L., Van Der Kolk, B. A., & Hoke, L. A. (1990) . Psychotherapy and psychological trauma in borderline personality disorder. Psychiatric Annals, 20(1), 33-43.

62.   Guzder, J., Paris, J., Selkowitz, P., & Feldman, R. (1999). Psychological risk factors for borderline pathology in school-age children. Journal of the American Academy of Child & Adolescent Psychiatry, 38 (2), 206-212.

63.   Zanarini, M. C., Gunderson, J. G., Marino, M. F., Schwartz, E. O., & Frankenburg, F. R. (1989) . Childhood experiences of borderline patients. Comprehensive Psychiatry, 30(1), 18-25.

64.   Zanarini, M.C., Williams, A.A., Lewis, R.E., Reich, R.B., Vera, S.C., Marino, M.F., Levin, A., Yong, L., & Frankenburg, F.R. (1998). Reported pathological childhood experiences associated with the development of borderline personality disorder. American Journal of Psychiatry, 154 (8), 1101-1106.

65.   Zanarini, M.C., Frankenburg, F.R., Reich, D.B., Marino, M.F., Haynes, M.C. & Gunderson, J.G. (1999). Biolence in the lives of adult borderline patients. Journal of Nervous and Mental Disease, 187 (2), 65-71.

66.   Dubo, E.D., Zanarini, M.C., Lewis, R.E., & Williams, A.A. (1997). Childhood antecedents of self-destructiveness in borderline personality disorder. Canadian Journal of Psychiatry, 42 (1), 63-69.

67.   Loranger, A. W., Oldham, J. M., & Utlis, E. H. (1982) . Familial transmission of DSM-III borderline personality disorder. Archives of General Psychiatry. 39, 795-799.

68.   Loranger, A. W. & Tulis, E. H. (1985). Family history of alcoholism in borderline personality disorder. Archives of General Psychiatry. 42, 153-157.

69.   Soloff, P. H. Millward, J. W. (1983). Psychiatric disorders in the families of borderline patients. Archives of General Psychiatry. 40, 37-44.

70.   Pope, H. G., Jonas, J. M., & Hudson, J. I. et.al. (1983). The validity of DSM-III personality disorder. Archives of General Psychiatry. 40, 23-30.

71.   Zanarini, M. C. Genderson, J. F., & Marinio, J. F. et.al. (Eds.) (1990). Psychiatric disorders in the families of borderline outpatients. Family Environment and Borderline Personality Disorder. Washington, D.C.: American Psychiatric Press.

72.   Kernberg, O. F., Selzer, M. A., Koenigsberg, H. W., Carr, A. C., Appelbaum, A. H. (1989). Psychodynamic Psychotherapy of Borderline Patients. New York: Basic Books.

73.   Sullivan, H.S. (1953). The interpersonal theory of psychiatry. New York: Norton.

74.   Pollack, W.S. (1986). Borderline personality disorder: Definition, diagnosis, assessment and treatment considerations. Innovations in clinical practice, 5, 103-135.

75.   Bryer, J. B., Nelson, B. A., Miller, F. B., & Krol, P. A. (1987). Childhood sexual and physical abuse as factors in adult psychiatric illness. American Journal of Psychiatry, 144, 1426-1430.

76.   Kernberg, O. F. (Eds.) (1982). Supportive psychotherapy with borderline conditions. Critical Problems in Psychiatry. Philadelphia: Lippincott.

77.   Adler, G. (1985). Borderline psychopathology and its treatment. New York: Aronson.

78.   Piper, W.E., Rosie, J.S., Azim, H.F.A., & Joyce, A.S. (1993). A randomized trial of psychiatric day treatment for patients with affective and personality disorders. Hospital Community Psychiatry, 44, 757-763.

79.   Kernberg, O. F., Bernstein, E., Coyne L. et.al. (1972). Psychotherapy and psychoanalysis: final report of the Menninger foundation's psychotherapy research project. Bulletin of the Menninger Clinic. 36(1), 275.

80.   Waldinger R. J., Gunderson, J. F. (1984). Completed psychotherapies with borderline patients. American Journal of Psychotherapy. 38(1), 90-201.

81.   Wallerstein (1986). Forty-two lives in treatment: A study of psychoanalysis and psychotherapy. New York: Guilford Press.

82.   Higgit, A. and Fonagy, P. (1992). Psychotherapy in borderline and narcissistic personality disorder. British Journal of Psychiatry, 161, 23-43.

83.   Stern, M.I., Herron, W.G., Primavera, L.H., & Kakuma, T. (1997). Interpersonal perceptions of depressed and borderline inpatients. Journal of Clinical Psychology, 53 (1), 41-49.

84.   Bateman, A., & Fonagy, P. (1999). Effectiveness of partial hospitalizaion in the treatment of borderline personality disorder: A randomized controlled trial. American Journal of Psychiatry, 156 (10), 1563-1569.

85.   Stevenson, J. & Meares, R. (1992). An outcome study of psychotherapy for patients with borderline personality disorder. American Journal of Psychiatry. 149(3), 358-362.

86.   Anchin, J. C. and Kiesler, D. J. (1982). The handbook of interpersonal psychotherapy. Elmsford, NY: Pergamon Press.

87.   Coley, C. H. (1956). Human nature and the social order. Glencoe, IL: Free Press

88.   Benjamin, L. S. (1974). Structural analysis of social behavior. Psychological Review, 81, 392-425.

89.   Benjamin, L.S. (1993). Interpersonal diagnosis and treatment of personality disorders. New York, N.Y.: Guilford Press.

90.   Shea et. al. (1990). National institute of mental health multicentre trial of treatment for affective disorders. American Journal of Psychiatry, 147, 711-718.

91.   Beck, A. T. & Arthur Freeman & Associates (1990). Cognitive therapy of personality disorders. New York: Guilford publications.

92.   Linehan, M. M. (1987). Dialectical behavior therapy for borderline personality disorder: Theory and methods. Bulletin of the Menninger Clinic, 51, 261-276.

93.   Linehan, M.M. & Kehrer, C.A. (1993). Borderline personality Disorder. In D.H. Barlwo (Ed.), Clinical Handbook of Psychological Disorders (2nd ed.) New York: Guilford Press, 396-441

94.   Heard, H.L. & Linehan, M.M. (1994). Dialectical behavior therapy: An integrative approach to the treatment of borderline personality disorder. Journal of Psychotherapy Integration, 4 (1), 55-82.

95.   Linehan, M.M. & Schmidt, H. (1995). The dialectics of effective treatment of borderline personality disorder. In W.O. O'Donohue & L. Krasner (Eds.), Theories in Behavior Therapy. Washington, D.C.: American Psychological Association, 553-584.

96.   Lewis, M. & Haviland, J. M. (Eds.) (1993). Handbook of emotions. New York: Guilford Press.

97.   Linehan, M.M. (1993). Cognitive-behavioral treatment of borderline personality disorder. New York: Guilford Press.

98.   Kastenbaum, J. F. (Eds.) (1969). Death and bereavement in later life. Death and bereavement. Springfield, IL: Charles C. Thomas.

99.   Linehan, M.M., Armstrong, H.E., Suearez, A., Allmon, D., & Heard, H.L. (1991). Cognitive-behavioral treatment of chronically parasuicidal borderline patients. Archives of General Psychiatry, 48, 1060-1064.

100.   Linehan, M.M, Tutek, K., & Heard, H.L. (1992). Interpersonal and social treatment outcomes for borderline personality disorder. Poster presented at the annual meeting of the Association of the Advancement of Behavior Therapy, Boston, MA.

101.   Linehan, M.M., Heard, H.L. & Armstrong, H.E. (1992). Naturalistic follow-up of a behavioral treatment for chronically parasuicidal borderline patients. Unpublished manuscript, University of Washington, Seattle, WA.

102.   Linehan, M.M., Tutek, D.A., Heard, H.L., & Armstrong, H.E. (1994). Interpersonal outcome of cognitive behavioral treatment for chronically suicidal borderline patients. The American Journal of Psychiatry, 151 (12), 1771-1776.

103.   Scheel, K.R. (2000). The emperical basis of dialectical behavior therapy: Summary, critique, and implications. Clinical Psychology: Science and Practice, 7, 68-86.

104.   Ryle, A. (1997). The structure and development of borderline personality disorder: A proposed model. British Journal of Psychiatry, 170, 82-87.

105.   Ryle, A., Leighton, T., & Pollock, P. (1997). Cognitive analytic therapy and borderline personality disorder: The model and the method. Chichister, England UK: John Wiley & Sons, Inc.

106.   Ryle, A. (2000). Effectiveness of time-limited cognitive analytic therapy of borderline personaltiy disorder: Factors associated with outcome. British Journal of Medical Psychology, 73 (pt2), 197-210.

107.   Ryle, A. (1997). The structure and development of borderline personality disorder: A proposed model. British Journal of Psychiatry, 170, 82-87.

108.   Parry, G. (1998). The accuracy of reformulation in cognitive analytic therapy: A validation study. Psychotherapy Research, 8 (1), 84-103.

109.   Marlett, G. A. & Gordon, J. R. (1985). Relapse prevention. New York: Guilford Press.

110.   Waldinger, R.J. (1986). Fundamentals of Psychiatry. Washington, D.C.: American Psychiatric Association.

111.   Clarkin, J. F., Koenigsberg, H., Yeomans, F. et.al. (1992). Psychodynamic psychotherapy of the borderline patient in Borderline Personality Disorder, Ed's Clarkin, J.F., Marziali, E., & Munroe-Blum, H. New York: Guilford Press.

112.   McIntyre, S.M., & Scwartz, R.C. (1998). Therapists' differential countertransference reactions toward clients with major depression or borderline personality disorder. Journal of Clinical Psychology, 54 (7), 923-931.

113.   Yalom, I. D. (1985) . The theory and practice of group psychotherapy. New York: Basic Books.

114.   Clarkin, J. F., Marziali, E., & Munroe-Blum, H. (1991). Group and family treatments for borderline personality disorder. Hospital and Community Psychiatry. 42(10), 1038-1043.

115.   Munroe-Blum, H., & Marziali, E. (1991). Time-limited group treatment of borderline personality disorder.

116.   Linehan, M. M. (1987b). Dialectical behavior therapy: A cognitive behavioral approach to parasuicide. Journal of Personality Disorders, 1, 328-333.

117.   Nehls, N. (1991). Borderline Personality Disorder and Group Therapy. Archives of Psychiatric Nursing, 3, 137-146.

118.   Soloff, P. H.. & Millward, J. W. (1983). Developmental histories of borderline patients. Comprehensive Psychiatry, 24, 547-588.

119.   Korzekwa, M., Links, P., and Steiner, M. (1993). Biological markers in borderline personality disorder: New perspectives. American Journal of Psychiatry, 38 (Suppl. 1), S11-15.

120.   Coccaro, E. F. & Kavoussi, R. J. (1991). Biological and pharmacological aspects of borderline personality disorder. Hospital and Community Psychiatry, 42(10), 1029-1034.

121.   Hirschfeld, R.M., (1997). Pharmacotherapy of borderline personality disorder. Journal of Clinical Psychiatry, 58 (suppl 14), 48-52.

122.   Coccaro, E.F. (1998). Clinical outcome of psychopharmacologic treatment of borderline and schizotypal personality disordered subjects. Journal of Clinical Psychiatry, 59 (suppl 1), 30-35.

123.   Steinberg, B.J., Trestman, R., Mitropoulou, V., Serby, M., Silverman, J., Coccaro, E., Weston, S., de Vegvar, M., & Siever, L.J. (1997). Depressive response to physostigmine challenge in borderline personality disorder patients. Neuropsychopharmacology, 17 (4), 264-273.

124.   Judd, P. H., & Ruff, R. M. (1993). Neuropsychological dysfunction in borderline personality disorder. Journal of Personality Disorders, 7(4), 275-284.

125.   Brown, G.L., Ebert, J.H., Goyer, P.F., Jimerson, D.C., Klein, W.J., Bunney, W.E. & Goodwin, F.K. (1982). Aggression, suicide & serotonin: Relationships to CSF amine metabilites. American Journal of Psychiatry, 139 (6), 741-746.

126.   Verkes, R. J., Van der Mast, R.C., Kerkhof, A.J., Fekkes, D., Hengeveld, M.W., Tuyl, J.P., & Van Kempen, G. M. (1998). Platelet serotonin, monoamine oxidase activity, and [3H] paroxetine binding related to impulsive suicide attempts and borderline personality disorder. Biological Psychiatry, 43 (10), 740-746.

127.   Choatai, J., Kullgren, G., & Asberg, M. (1998). CSF monoamine metabolites in relation to the diagnostic interview for borderline patients (DIB). Neuropsychobiology, 38 (4), 207.212.

128.   De la Fuente, J.M., Tugendhaft, P., & Mavroudakis, N. (1998). Electroencephalographic abnormalities in borderline personality disorder. Psychiatry Research, 77 (2), 131-138.

129.   Soloff, P.H. (1994). Is there any drug treatment of choice for the borderline patient? Acta Psychiatric Scandinavia, 89(Suppl. 379), 50-55.

130.   Bradley, S. S. (1990). Nonphysician psychotherapist-physician pharmacotherapist: A new model for concurrent treatment. <u>Psychiatric Clinics of North America,</u> <u>13</u>(2), 307-321.

131.   Silva, H., Jerez, S., Paredes, A., Salvo, J., Reneria, P., Ramirez, A., & Montes, C. (1997). Fluoxetine in the treatment of borderline personality disorder. <u>Actas Luso-Espanolas de Neurologia, Psiquiatria Y Ciencias Afines,</u> <u>25</u> (6), 391-395.

132.   Chengappa, K.N.R., Ebeling, T., Kang, J.S., Levine, J., & Parepally, H. (1999). Clozapine reduces severe self-mutilation and aggression in psychotic patients with borderline personality disorder. <u>Journal of Clinical Psychiatry,</u> <u>60</u> (7), 477-484.

133.   Bendetti, F., Sforzini, L., Colombo, C., Marrei, C., & Smeraldi, E. (1998). Low-dose clozapine in acute and continuation treatment of severe borderline personality disorder. <u>Journal of Clinical Psychiatry,</u> <u>59</u> (3), 103-107.

134.   Bohus, M.J., Landwehrmeyer, G.B., Stiglmayr, C.E., Limberger, M.F., Bohme, R., & Schmahl, C.G. (1999). Naltrexone in the treatment of dissociative symptoms in patients with borderline personality disorder: An open-label trial. <u>Journal of Clinical Psychiatry,</u> <u>60</u> (9), 598-603.

Index

© Compact Clinicals

We Want Your Opinion!

Comments about the book: _____

Name of Book

_____

_____

_____

_____

Other titles you want Compact Clinicals to offer:

_____

_____

_____

Please provide your name and address in the space below to be placed on our mailing list.

_____

_____

_____

_____

Compact Clinicals

Ordering in three easy steps:

1 **Please fill out completely:**

Billing/Shipping Information

Individual/Company _____ Department/Mail Stop _____

Profession _____

Street Address/P.O. Box _____

City, State, Zip _____

Telephone _____ ☐ Ship to residence ☐ Ship to business

2 **Here's what I'd like to order:**

Book Name	Book Qty.	Unit Price	Total
Aggressive and Defiant Behavior The Latest Assessment and Treatment Strategies for the Conduct Disorders		$14.95	
Attention Deficit Hyperactivity Disorder (in Adults and Children) The Latest Assessment and Treatment Strategies		$14.95	
Borderline Personality Disorder The Latest Assessment and Treatment Strategies		$14.95	
Depression in Adults The Latest Assessment and Treatment Strategies		$14.95	
Obsessive Compulsive Disorder The Latest Assessment and Treatment Strategies		$14.95	
Post-Traumatic Stress Disorder The Latest Assessment and Treatment Strategies		$14.95	

Subtotal	
Tax Add (6.85% in MO)	
Shipping Fee Add ($3.75 for the first book and $1.00 for each additional book)	
Total Amount	

Continuing Education credits available for mental health professionals. Call 1-800-408-8830 for details.

3 **Payment Method:** Telephone Orders/Toll Free: 1(800)408-8830 • Fax Orders to: 1(816)587-7198

Send Postal Orders to: Compact Clinicals • 7205 NW Waukomis Dr., Suite A • Kansas City, MO 64151

☐ Check Enclosed

☐ Please charge to my:

○ Visa   Name on Card _____

○ MasterCard   Cardholder Signature _____

○ Discover Card   Account #/Exp. Date _ _ _ _ - _ _ _ _ - _ _ _ _ - _ _ _ _ (_ _/_ _)

We Want Your Opinion!

Comments about the book: _____

Name of Book

_____

_____

_____

_____

Other titles you want Compact Clinicals to offer:

_____

_____

_____

_____

Please provide your name and address in the space below to be placed on our mailing list.

_____

_____

_____

_____

Compact Clinicals

Ordering in three easy steps:

1 **Please fill out completely:**

Billing/Shipping Information

Individual/Company   Department/Mail Stop

Profession

Street Address/P.O. Box

City, State, Zip

Telephone   ☐ Ship to residence   ☐ Ship to business

2 **Here's what I'd like to order:**

Book Name	Book Qty.	Unit Price	Total
Aggressive and Defiant Behavior The Latest Assessment and Treatment Strategies for the Conduct Disorders		$14.95	
Attention Deficit Hyperactivity Disorder (in Adults and Children) The Latest Assessment and Treatment Strategies		$14.95	
Borderline Personality Disorder The Latest Assessment and Treatment Strategies		$14.95	
Depression in Adults The Latest Assessment and Treatment Strategies		$14.95	
Obsessive Compulsive Disorder The Latest Assessment and Treatment Strategies		$14.95	
Post-Traumatic Stress Disorder The Latest Assessment and Treatment Strategies		$14.95	

Subtotal	
Tax Add (6.85% in MO)	
Shipping Fee Add ($3.75 for the first book and $1.00 for each additional book)	
Total Amount	

Continuing Education credits available for mental health professionals. Call 1-800-408-8830 for details.

3 **Payment Method:** Telephone Orders/Toll Free: 1(800)408-8830 • Fax Orders to: 1(816)587-7198
Send Postal Orders to: Compact Clinicals • 7205 NW Waukomis Dr., Suite A • Kansas City, MO 64151

☐ Check Enclosed
☐ Please charge to my:

○ Visa   Name on Card

○ MasterCard   Cardholder Signature

○ Discover Card   Account #/Exp. Date   _ _ _ _ - _ _ _ _ - _ _ _ _ - _ _ _ _ (_ _/_ _)